Sun Tzu & Machiavelli Leadership Secrets

How to Become a Superior Leader Utilizing the Principles of The Art Of War And The Prince

By Anthony D. Jensen

D1310928

Table of Contents

Introduction - Meet The Masters 5

Chapter 1 - Know Your War 8

Chapter 2 - Sun Tzu's Five Factors For Superior Leadership..12

Chapter 3 - Deception & Perception - Your Secret Weapons 17

Chapter 4 - Be Rapid and Resourceful 30

Chapter 5 - Dissent Is Death 41

Chapter 6 - Independence Is Strength 52

Chapter 7 - Know What Is Necessary 62

Chapter 8 - Embrace Chaos and Expect The Unexpected...72

Chapter 9 - Protect What's Yours................................82

Chapter 10 - Consider The Consequences..................92

Chapter 11 - Win Flawless Victories Before Fighting 102

Chapter 12 - Eternal Invulnerability..........................114

Chapter 13 - Know When To Push And Pull............124

Chapter 14 - Strategic Study 134

Chapter 15 - Be Like Water To Drown Your Enemies 144

Chapter 16 - Respect Every Territory 154

Chapter 17 - Master Morale And Earn Respect.......164

Chapter 18 - The Power Of No....................................174

Chapter 19 - Don't Nail Your Own Coffin 184

Chapter 20 - Emphasize The Extraordinary............194

Chapter 21 - The Ripple Effect...................................204

Chapter 22 - Advisors & Intelligence........................215

Chapter 23 - Attack By Fire..225

Introduction - Meet The Masters

Sun Tzu's 'The Art of War' and Machiavelli's 'The Prince' are two classical works on power, influence and leadership which have been key guides for some of the most powerful leaders since their publication.

Leaders of all types - whether CEOs of major international companies, head coaches of Super Bowl winning NFL teams or military generals have made use of the advice found within the works of Sun Tzu and Machiavelli.

One of the most common reasons that people fail to make use of these two vital strains of classical thought is the difficulty in understanding the original texts. Both were written in languages other than English and for a time and place different to our own.

The Update

This book represents a combination of the most powerful ideas found in The Art of War, and The Prince, but updated and applied to the modern context.

Areas of agreement between the two master thinkers are identified and expanded upon. Ultimately, this book presents the key ideas in a way which has never been easier to use and understand.

The Application

Almost any area of life can be improved by the application of the ideas this book contains - your career, your private life and your interpersonal relationships. Anywhere that power is needed to attain an outcome can be helped by applying Machiavellian thought.

As you read through this book, it is vital to keep in mind how you will apply the ideas contained within. There is no point in reading this book simply as a set of theoretical ideas - it is useful only as a set of actions which must be actually applied to real life.

The most common examples in the book are situations within the world of corporate business and also within the sphere of your personal aims and objectives. However, if you look at the underlying ideas and concepts, you will be able to come up with a range of applications that are suited to your own unique circumstances and objectives.

<u>Be Prepared</u>

This book will challenge your notions of power and influence. Morality is not the focus of this work - only effectiveness. You must be open-minded. What you read may shock you. Be warned.

Chapter 1 - Know Your War

One area of leadership which was emphasized by both Machiavelli and Sun Tzu, and also received backing from modern leadership theory, is the need to start with the end in mind. As a leader, you need to know your intended outcome in any given situation. Without having a clear idea of what you want to get from a situation, you will never be able to guide your every action and every decision towards this aim.

Every course of action you take in life needs to be seen as a war. Why? Simply put, you will be exerting effort, expending resources, and there is likely to be a winner and a loser. Not every war is violent. Some wars you will be able to win without fighting. You need to take every situation as serious and give it the respect it deserves. Only by viewing every war as unique will you be able to put into place the right course of action to lead you to your aim.

Look Back As Well As Forward

Machiavelli, writing in The Prince, stated that seeing things as a war requires to look forward as well as back. Machiavelli used the example of taking control of one area which was previously free and one which was not. The approach needed to rule over each effectively would be different. It is not enough to only look forward but it is vital to think in terms of what has gone before. We can only shape the future of a situation when we first understand its past.

Make Your War Winnable

It is not enough for an effective leader to know only the path they wish to walk - they need to know where it ends. The worst war, in the eyes of both Machiavelli and Sun Tzu, is the one without an end. Committing time and financial resources to something which does not have a clear stopping point is one of the most inefficient courses of action possible.

It is also important to know that simply knowing what the end is does not mean that you will be able to get there. There are some wars which we are not able to win, no matter how well we pursue them. Knowing which wars are winnable before getting involved in them is something which will be dealt with in later chapters. For now, it is enough to know that something must offer the likelihood of victory to be worth pursuing.

Your Life Is War

The book will offer a mix of organizational and personal examples of the ideas of Machiavelli and Sun Tzu. It is important to realize that every concept which is detailed has application and utility within your personal life as well.

The main problem people make in their personal life is failing to understand that life is not some utopian fairy story in which doing the right, ethical things will always lead people to the best outcomes. This book challenges you to take control of your life and always see things through one lens and one lens only - the willingness to do whatever it takes.

Get Ready For War

The following chapters will explore various, in-depth aspects of preparing for, going to and, ultimately, winning the many wars your life will consist of. For now, it is enough for you to know that every area of your life is one which you must face full-on and with a commitment to victory.

The only question is whether you are ready to fight?

Chapter 2 - Sun Tzu's Five Factors For Superior Leadership

We will now briefly explore the five factors Sun Tzu saw as essential for effective leadership. Each of these is expanded upon in subsequent chapters. For now, understand they provide an oversight of the types of factors you will need to make use of in order to achieve your aims as a leader.

The Way

The Way refers to how essential it is to command a unified force. Everyone needs to be pulling in the same direction and do whatever it takes in order to succeed. Those you lead must be willing to do whatever you ask of them and do so without question.

Later in this book, you will be shown the importance of exercising total and utter control over the people you lead. Absolutely unity of purpose between your aims, the aims of an organization and the aims of the people you lead will be shown to be a vital prerequisite for victory.

Heaven

Heaven refers to the less firm aspects of victory - aspects such as yin and yang and the alternating of seasons. These can be understood as the elements outside of a leader's direct control. Machiavelli also states that luck and factors outside of our control have a role in any outcome.

Grasping the intangible factors at play in any given situation is difficult as they are less apparent. This book makes use of a Machiavellian concept related to protecting against the nature of fortune and luck in order to enhance Sun Tzu's understanding of the heavenly aspects of victory.

Earth

Earth refers to the conditions on the ground which enable victory to occur. This relates to such aspects of the type of territory held, the ease and difficulty of it, and the layout of the terrain. These aspects will all be explored more fully in later chapters.

In the times of Sun Tzu, territory and terrain were referred to in the literal senses of the terms - they related to physical battlefields and actual, direct, violent warfare. In the modern context, terrain and territory are often used in an analogous sense. This book will show how the traditional notions of terrain and territory are equally applicable to the modern leader as they were to those in antiquity.

Command

Command is the extent to which a leader is wise, practices integrity, shows compassion where it is wise to, has the courage to pursue their own decisions and is able to act with sufficient severity when needed.

Figuring out the time to show different sides of your nature as a leader is one of the hardest aspects to master. The book makes use of various examples and ideas from the Art of War and The Prince to show that a one size fits all approach to command is not the best way to be. Instead, it is vital for the modern effective leader to adapt their approach to whatever is needed at the time.

Discipline

Discipline refers to the structure and rigidity which is in place on behalf of a leader in order for his intentions to be carried out. This refers to strict orders, strict rules and other elements needed to ensure action is as efficient as possible.

Discipline is often the difference between success and failure in the modern world. It is more fashionable than ever for leaders to employ a very loose, almost laissez-faire view of leadership, this book advocates a return to ruthless, traditional ways of leading in order to secure a competitive advantage over rivals who have been weakened by the modern way.

Comparing The Five Factors

Sun Tzu states that it is possible to determine who will win in advance by comparing the five factors. It is important to always see situations in terms of the factors at play, and which side compares more favorably against the other. Later chapters will enable you to understand each of the five factors in greater detail, and combines them with Machiavellian wisdom in order to provide the most powerful leadership methods ever thought up.

Chapter 3 - Deception & Perception - Your Secret Weapons

Ultimately, Sun Tzu and Machiavelli both discuss power. They do this in different ways and have different areas of emphasis, but the bottom line is that both sets of ideas are based on gaining, maintaining and exercising power. As a leader, power can seem like an abstract concept that is difficult to grasp and put into actionable ideas. Two very actionable concepts appear as key themes in both The Art of War and The Prince - deception and perception. This chapter explores how being able to strategically deploy deception in a range of situations can lead to a significant advantage for leaders. It also shows how being able to control, influence and even manipulate perception is a vital part of powerful leadership.

<u>Sun Tzu's Deception - Updated and Applied</u>

Let's take a look at some of the ways that Sun Tzu spoke of deception in The Art of War and how these can be interpreted and understood in the modern era.

"When able to attack, seem unable" is one of the most famous sections of The Art of War.

This was originally meant in the context of military endeavors. Indeed, even in the modern era, many military forces make use of Sun Tzu's text directly to influence their approach to warfare. The idea of attack does not have to be literal however. So how can we understand attack outside of combat?

Essentially, we can apply the idea of 'attack' in the sense of 'an aggressive or outgoing course of action'. Think of the term 'plan of attack' - it does not literally have to be violent. With this new, non-literal definition of attack in mind, what are some of the ways we can apply Sun Tzu's famous maxim?

Personal Attacks

One of the key applications of seeming unable to attack is within the personal sphere of career and business. Many corporate environments feature a range of highly coveted promotions that are known about and sought after by many. This is where the entire concept of 'office politics' comes from. Even the most mundane office environment is likely to have a range of rivalries and dramas. Almost anyone who has ever worked in the modern era will be aware of the focus of these dynamics - rivals trying to suss each other out, pull off feats of one upmanship, and look better than their foes.

Guess what? The most effective way to attack is to do so when no-one sees it coming. If you are going for a promotion, keep it as secret as possible. If you are not perceived as a threat, as a challenger, you will be off the radar in terms of competition. If you are targeting someone's job, keep it secret. They will never know your attack is coming and will be unable to defend themselves against your intentions in time.

Large Scale Attacks

The idea of hiding your intention to attack, so your targets are unprepared, does not just apply on a small scale, personal level. It also works on a larger scale, such as the actions and strategic plans of an entire organization. This concept is easy to illustrate with an example - Apple product launches.

Think about the drama and excitement that comes with the launch of a new Apple product. People speculate like crazy about what the new unveiling will bring. Apple is as secretive as possible ahead of time. Then, on the day of the launch, the product is revealed and usually announced to be on sale within a very short period of time. As a result of this, competitors are on the backfoot. They never know exactly what is coming and what they should do as a result. The launch of the original iPhone was a game changer - Apple did not necessarily seem set to attack the portion of the tech market that they chose. As a result of this, competing firms had no real time to prepare. Look at the fates of Blackberry and Motorola if you doubt this concept.

Stealth

Another famous quote on deception from The Art of War states 'when using forces, seem inactive'. This is more true than ever these days. We live in an era where people are encouraged to broadcast their every thought, plan and intention through social media. Countless cases of people being caught out in terms of identity fraud, affairs, or going against workplace rules, have come to light because of people not being cautious enough. If you work quietly and behind the scenes, you have a significant advantage over those who do not.

One of the key areas in which working behind the scenes can work is politics - both in the electoral sense and in general. Often, politicians focus heavily on preparing their views, appearance and perception in a way which makes them seem favorable in comparison to a known rival, then out of nowhere, a little known challenger will make a massive push and catch the favorites off guard. It's not as if the newcomer started overnight - they likely began to work diligently and quietly a long time before. They just had the good sense to not make a big deal of what they were doing, which would give their rivals a chance to prepare and take countermeasures.

It is not enough to just act quietly - it is sometimes vital to seem specifically inactive. This can be done through sleight of hand. Let's say, for example, a skill is valued in a workplace. A number of people are working hard to acquire this skill in the hope of advancing up the career ladder. Someone is also acquiring this skill - but in secret. They not only do this secretly, but make a point of seeming to be uninterested or uninvolved whenever the topic of the new skill arises. This is an example of proactively hiding one's efforts in order to gain a strategic advantage.

The Illusion Of Distance

'When near, make the enemy believe you are far away' states The Art of War. This is a powerful concept which can be applied in a number of fields.

Human beings have evolved to be conscious of the immediate and obvious threats to their safety and prosperity. If something is obviously dangerous and nearby, our guard goes up and our defenses heighten. If something seems like a distant prospect, however, we are less worried by it at the time. Let's look at modern warfare to show how this works.

Take two modern situations - the conflict in Korea between the North and South, and the ongoing threat of terrorism. In Korea, the threat is obvious and near. Troops are amassed on either side of the border and there is a constant awareness of the potential for conflict. Both sides are prepared and ready, and therefore are in something of a stalemate. Terrorism, on the other hand, remains under the radar. There is no formal membership structure. People assume they are safe and then, suddenly, a bomb goes off. The proximity of the threat is unknown at any given time and therefore cannot be adequately expected.

So what are some of the non-violent uses of strategic deception relating to proximity?

Market entry is one area of business where seeming to be distant can provide an advantage. If you wish to enter a new market, such as a region, then it may be useful to prepare to do so quietly and discretely. If your competitors don't know you are close to entering a market, their attention is not drawn to it. They are unlikely to assume the market is worthy of consideration as a result of your interest in it.

The Power Of Machiavellian Perception

One of the key recurring themes in The Prince is that a leader can get away with almost anything if he appears to be a certain way in the eyes of the masses. Therefore, almost any true nature can be covered up by careful management of perception. Numerous examples show this is as true in the modern day as it was in the time of Machiavelli.

Countless corporations are adept at using marketing to seem as if they are ethical or praiseworthy in some way or another while secretly pursuing entirely different motives. Politicians are another prime example of this idea. How many candidates running for office, or even prominent politicians, have claimed to be wholesome and family friendly and then have been exposed to be engaged in infidelity or some other form of vice?

Interestingly, often, even when someone or something's true nature is exposed, many people will still rush to defend it. Why? The person or entity in question was so skilled at using perception to appear a certain way, while being another, that the false perception is deeply embedded in people's minds. People hate feeling like they have been duped, so will do almost anything to cling on to the false image they held. Think of the countless celebrities who have been caught out as doing disgraceful acts but still command legions of fans who claim the individuals in question were simply 'misunderstood'. Perception is powerful - use it to your advantage.

Keeping a true behavior or nature hidden is harder in the modern era than it ever has been.

Think of the countless examples of old photographs or emails giving the game away. Even old data can be hacked and released into the public to devastating effect. It is therefore absolutely vital that anything that you wish to remain hidden is kept in the utmost secrecy. Stay away from email, text messages, social media - anything that could come back to haunt you. Conduct your true plans in secrecy and away from any chance of ever being exposed.

While doing one thing in secret, it's important to leave a trail of doing something different, and acceptable in the eyes of the public, publicly. Let's say, for example, as a manager you need to get rid of one of your workers. You know you must plot their downfall in secret. It's not enough to plot and scheme behind closed doors - you must appear to be very fair, even on the doomed worker's side, in public. If done skillfully enough, they will eventually feel almost bad for you when you fire them, as you will seem like a true friend who had their back. Really, their demise was inevitable the entire time.

Deception and Perception - Sun Tzu and Machiavelli Combined

Like many powerful concepts, deception and perception are more potent together than apart. If you take away one core idea from this chapter, it should be that it is not enough to actively do one thing in secret - you need to put out false information and seem to be doing something very different in the eyes of the masses.

To really apply the ideas in this chapter, always keep two ideas in mind.

1. Which parts of my current course of action should I do in secret?
2. How can I appear to be doing something differently to others?

It's also important to always remain aware of the variables in any given situation. A form of deception that worked once might not work again. Other chapters discuss the importance of adaptability in greater depth - for now just be aware that your manipulation of deception and perception should be unique to be effective.

Chapter 4 - Be Rapid and Resourceful

Much of the modern leadership literature focuses on concepts such as waste, efficiency and the protracted cost of doing business in adverse circumstances. For example, waste is a common theme in quality improvement literature. It can be argued that Sun Tzu focused on efficiency and prudent management a long time before such notions were popular. One of the key teachings in The Art of War is avoiding protracted conflict. Like many of Sun Tzu's concepts, it can be updated and used in the modern era without meaning a literal aggressive conflict.

Modern Protracted Wars

In order to think about the idea of a protracted conflict in a way which is useful for the modern era, think of it as any unusual situation which expends effort and resources at a rate which is more rapid than usual. A few examples of concrete situations which consist of modern protracted wars will now be expanded upon.

Personal situations are one way in which a modern protracted war can be seen as undesirable. Some situations which consist of a modern protracted war include putting in more hours than normal into a project, acquiring a new skill or traveling excessively. Basically, any unusual activity which saps energy, time or other resources in a more than usual manner can be seen as a personal protracted conflict.

Sometimes, it is necessary to enter into a situation which will drain your time or resources. Before taking such a course of action, however, a few things need to be clearly established. First, it must be considered whether the rewards of the action will be equal or greater to the resources expended in order to acquire it. Second, it should be considered whether some other, less taxing course of action could result in the same benefits. Finally, if the protracted personal war is seen as beneficial or unavoidable, it should be considered whether there are any ways to mitigate the negative effects.

Shorten The War

Often, in the case of personal wars, there will be a way to achieve victory faster than it initially seemed. Let's use the example of acquiring a skill or studying to explore this example. Traditional methods of learning are often inefficient or more lengthy than they need to be. Think of a traditional college degree, for example. This takes a number of years. Of those years, how often are the students away from the learning environment? While they are learning, how much is actually useful? Think of the massive inefficiencies and delays that occur. It is almost always possible to take the useful aspects of an education program and absorb them in a fraction of the time.

One of the best ways to see if a protracted personal war can be shortened is to find a role model who was able to achieve results in a more rapid than usual way. Their techniques and tips can be modeled, applied and used to reduce the wastage and expended resources that would have been needed to achieve the aim in the traditional way.

Large Scale Protracted Wars

The modern take on a protracted war can be applied to a more macro context than the personal, individual aims and objectives. Often, organizations, families or other groups of people will be engaged in something that is drawn out and costly for as long as it lasts. Let's take a look at some examples of protracted wars in the context of a modern business organization.

Perhaps the most common analogy to traditional wars in the modern time are the modern wars that take place between corporations. Price wars,

wars for market share, wars for talent - there are many ways in which large organizations clash against each other in the course of aiming to achieve their objectives. These take a toll on organizations in terms of the resources expended and also the opportunity cost of not being able to use their resources in another way.

Whatever the large scale conflict, it is almost always undesirable. It may be necessary to enter into a situation for a period of time. For example, if a newcomer enters the market, there may be no choice except to compete against them in order to crush their chances of success and survival. The key to choosing to enter a conflict is to have a clear objective and to end the conflict in the most rapid way possible.

Define Victory Before Going To War

One of the most important aspects of entering into a modern war, be it small or large scale, is to understand the purpose of taking action before beginning to do so. For example, if a person is going to have to work excess hours to get a project finished, they should have an absolute clear idea of what the finish line looks like. Failing to define victory in advance leaves either individuals or organizations open to getting stuck into an endless course of action and being unable to even envision when or how it will end.

One of the key reasons that cause people or companies to enter into a war without having a clear victory in mind is emotion, reaction or other similar factors. The only criteria for entering into a war should be based on cold, rational logic. There is no place to be hotheaded, rash or otherwise provoked into action. Any conflict should be freely chosen and under the most rational, calm circumstances possible. This avoids entering into costly situations without a clear reason for doing so.

Plan Rapidly For Every Situation

Life is chaotic and the pace of change can be fast. One mistake which often results in organizations or individuals becoming trapped in a long war is expecting things to go a certain way without considering the alternative possibilities. Let's say, for example, a company is launching a new product and competing directly against another organization. In such a circumstance, a key mistake would be to assume there is only one possible way other actors, such as customers or companies, could respond, and basing plans entirely on that expected course of action.

The better way to enter into a conflict scenario which has the potential to become drawn out is to plot out a range of different scenarios for what could occur and devise a course of action in the event of each. It is necessary to put every possibility on the table at first. Each possibility can then be assessed in terms of its likelihood and a course of response determined. So what are some of the ways of considering the various permutations of any given situation which may arise?

One important starting point when devising different scenarios is to look at the past. It is rare that something truly unique happens - there is almost always a precedent of one type or another. In the case of a company, it is vital to look at any time the company in question had attempted something similar in the past, and what the outcome was. It is also looking into the wider literature to determine the possible outcomes in similar scenarios. The same applies for individuals. The individuals must first consider their own personal history, and what the outcome was when facing similar challenges, and then look at other individuals and the type of things they have faced.

Once a range of possible scenarios have been explored, and the likelihood of them considered, it is useful to think about the response that would best counter any given outcome. It is not enough to only know 'a could happen, or b could happen'. It is vital to know 'if a happens, we will do x. If b happens, we will do y'. This means that an organization or individual stands a better chance of being prepared to respond to whatever takes place.

This scenario planning isn't perfect, of course. There will always be the potential for something unexpected to occur, or a variation on something expected which requires a different response. This in no way, however, means that scenario planning is a waste of time. When done properly, it anticipates and readies entities for what they may face. Even when something expected occurs, it allows for businesses and people to modify an existing plan to respond to the new challenge. This can help shorten the length of a war and avoid a protracted and costly conflict from spiraling out of control due to a lack of preparation.

Consider The Costs & Budget Accordingly

It is not enough to know which conflicts to enter, which to avoid and what a response would be in any given situation. It is important to know what costs will be faced in any given situation and how these will be met. When anticipating costs, it is important to always err on the side of conservatism and caution. It is also important to consider costs in different areas as well as total costs.

Some of the areas where costs might be incurred during a conflict include human costs, physical costs, financial costs and time costs. It is important to project how much cost in any given area will be incurred by each anticipated or considered course of action. It may be that a course of action is chosen due to an ability to meet costs in one area but not in another. Each individual or organization will have certain resources or competencies which enable them to be effective in some ways more than others. Matching a course of action to the ability to meet its costs is therefore a wise element of decision making.

One of Sun Tzu's key principles is to avoid incurring costs directly where possible. In his words, it is better to make the enemy pay than to pay ourselves. This advice is also useful for modern leadership. For example, always look to get resources from external sources. One powerful example of this is leveraged takeovers in which companies are purchased but loaded with debt.

Chapter 5 - Dissent Is Death

Sun Tzu and Machiavelli stress again and again throughout their works that obedience and a lack of dissent are absolutely vital conditions for effective leadership to occur. This is one area of leadership that many mistakenly feel is appropriate for the older times but not the modern world in which we live. A lot of people see a decisive, my way or the highway style of leadership as immoral or wrong for the time in which we live. This viewpoint couldn't be more wrong. Leading with absolute authority is not only vital to achieve effective results - it is actually kinder to the people you are leading to lead in this way.

The Necessity Of Authority

One of the most common mistakes modern leaders make is misunderstanding their role. Many leaders think they should somehow be friends or even 'family members' to those they lead. Think about 'The Office' for example. The TV show is a sign of how ineffectual leadership is when it fails to be authoritative and firm. People don't want to be led by some weak facsimile of a friend. Instead, people want, need and respond best to firm and decisive direction.

The problem of strong leadership in the modern time is people perhaps misunderstand what is meant by the concept. Being strong, decisive and obeyed does not mean that you have to be a parody of a dictator. Sun Tzu, more so than Machiavelli, emphasized that it was necessary for a leader to be the type of person who men wanted to fight for. Machiavelli also emphasized that it was not possible to treat those one lead unfairly, such as by taking their property or otherwise exploiting them, and still expect obedience and loyalty.

One reason why modern leaders are often afraid to be strong, decisive and commanding is due to the fact that they may have had success with taking a softer approach to leadership. After all, if a leader had been friendly and taken a soft touch to their responsibilities, why would they see the point of being stronger and tough? Interestingly, this was something that Machiavelli foresaw in The Prince.

Loved Or Feared?

If you asked the vast majority of modern leaders whether they would prefer to be loved or feared, almost all would state their preference to be loved. Why? People often see being loved as somehow more morally praiseworthy and even more effective. So what did Machiavelli have to say about the concept of being loved as a leader, and the moral dimension of love and fear as leadership techniques?

Interestingly, despite his reputation as almost evil, Machiavelli was an open minded thinker who did not have any preconceived notions about leadership, human beings and political influence. A careful reading of The Prince shows that Machiavelli was not concerned with seeing things in any certain way - instead he wanted only to see things for how they were. As part of this open minded exploration of influence, Machiavelli stated that it was possible to lead through love or fear, but it was better to be feared than loved.

The viewpoint that Machiavelli reached helps to explain why many modern leaders prefer to be loved than feared. First, Machiavelli did indeed recognize that love could motivate people to obey a leader and strive for their cause. Second, in our modern culture, the cultural norm is less inclined to look kindly upon strong and fearful leadership. Love is a more widely promoted cultural notion. So if love has been recognized as somewhat effective by Machiavelli, why is it better to be feared?

The first reason why fear is preferable to love, at least from a Machiavellian standpoint, is that there is no moral dimension to leadership. Machiavelli was not concerned with saying one style of leadership was morally right while another was morally wrong - instead he was concerned only with finding what was effective and produced results. This first point goes against the modern notion that it is somehow more inherently praiseworthy to be loved than feared. Machiavellian thought demolishes this notion and instead insists that it is vital only for leaders to produce results, not to worry about some nebulous moral dimension.

The second, and main reason, why Machiavelli states that it is better to be feared than loved is due to the fact that Machiavelli believed that people, and therefore their love, are fickle. Many leaders throughout the course of history have been loved. How many were loved forever? Very few. Even Winston Churchill, the loved wartime leader of the UK during World War 2, lost his popularity and was voted out of office in subsequent years. Love is not reliable and therefore cannot be relied upon in the long term to produce obedience and control. Fear is therefore the only reliable option for effective leadership.

The Wise General

One section of the The Art of War states 'The Wise General is a Lord of Destiny'. This statement is profound and is a huge justification and reason for the need for strong leadership, especially in the modern context. The statement may seem to be simple upon first glance, but it actually has a fair amount of depth and meaning when the time is taken to explore its layers.

First, let's look at the concept of a 'Wise General'. By referring to wisdom, Sun Tzu is stating that it is not enough to merely be a strong leader - one must also use their intellect, discretion and judgment to behave in a wise way. This helps to demolish the pejorative modern stereotype as being some kind of cartoon caveman figure who is unable to think clearly. Throughout history, wisdom and strength have gone hand in hand. Modern leaders would do well to return to this combination of traits during a time period in which their coexistence is scarce.

Sun Tzu went on to declare that a Wise General 'holds the nation's peace or peril in his hands'. This statement, above all others, should convince you of the need to exercise strong leadership, no matter what the situation is that you are leading. Failing to be strong, decisive and demanding of obedience will lead only to peril. Conversely, exercising strong leadership and being effective in commanding others, will help to bring peace and prosperity to whichever situation you are in control of.

'Peace and peril' is a concept which relates to far more than just the battlefield. If you are a leader within a company, no matter how many employees you lead, you should always keep in mind the idea of 'peace and peril'. The people you lead are relying on you for their jobs, their income and their families' security and safety. If you are not a strong leader then you are risking bringing chaos and misery into the lives of many.

'Peace and peril' is equally valid to areas of personal leadership. Many people think they should be gentle with themselves and not put too much pressure, stress and demand on their own lives. If you keep in mind the idea that your choice of how you lead your own life will lead to either a peaceful or a perilous existence then you may be less tempted to go easy on yourself. After all, your inner peace or your inner turmoil are at stake. When your own happiness is the spoils of war, lead yourself into your daily battles with nothing but strength, self-discipline and self-obedience.

Violence & Force To Crush Dissent

Machiavelli is keen to emphasize the need of using violence and force in order to establish a strong, obedient type of leadership. In the modern context, using literal violence is difficult due to legal constraints in almost any context. It is possible, however, to take forceful and ruthless action which has the same end product of obedience and fear as actual violence would have. Let's look at some of the ways in which forceful action can lead to a death of dissent.

The first key to crushing out dissent from what your leadership aims are is to make clear there are very clear consequences for going against you. This requires absolutely ruthless dedication to being strong on your behalf. If someone violates your rules, come down on them with full force. Make an example of them in front of others. Even be harsher than is needed in early instances. Machiavelli was keen to state that it is especially important to take decisive control as soon as entering into a new leadership situation.

Dissent is like a disease that can grow, spread and mutate the longer it is left unchallenged. Not a single second can be wasted if you notice dissent or disobedience occur. Crush it. This is equally as important in any given leadership situation - the workplace, personal leadership or even parenting. The basic principle is the same. If people disobey you, and there are no consequences, it not only makes it almost certain that the same people will disobey you in the future, but also makes it an almost certainty that others will choose to do the same. After all, if you are not the type of leader that is able to enforce their own wishes, why would people want to obey you?

Key Lessons

In summary, this chapter has shown the importance of establishing strong authority which is obeyed at all times. It has been recognized that both love and fear can be workable leadership styles, but fear is more reliable and effective. The responsibility of strong leadership has been shown to be a duty of the leader as peace or peril is the outcome of their choices. Finally, violence and force have been shown to be necessary tools in ensuring dissent is destroyed as soon as it starts.

Chapter 6 - Independence Is Strength

A key concern for both Machiavelli and Sun Tzu was exploring what exactly makes one leader strong and effective while another leader is neither of those things. One of the factors that both The Prince and The Art of War return to again and again is the need to be independent and self-reliant. This is a concept which both chimes with and goes against some of the ideas found in modern thinking. This chapter explores various aspects of independence, how to achieve them and how they help to make the modern leader effective.

You Are All You Have

The one constant in any of our lives is ourselves. Think about it. No matter what you think you have other than yourself, you are wrong. You can and eventually will lose everything and everyone around you. At first, this sounds somewhat bleak and depressing. In actual fact, it's incredibly empowering. When we realize that we are all we really have, we are free. We can put ourselves first and know that in doing so we are only strengthening our own position in life.

There are many ways in which modern leaders fail to realize they are all they have. In the case of smaller companies, many leaders mistake the purpose of their leadership and even of the company itself. Instead of seeing the company as a vehicle through which to make money, these misguided leaders begin to see it as some kind of family. They begin to see the workers for more than they are. They even begin to rely on the particular people who are around them. This is a recipe for absolute disaster. People come and go and relying on anyone or anything is a mistake. No-one, and nothing, are irreplaceable, and seeing them as such is a recipe for disaster. What happens when your irreplaceable employee quits or your unique machine breaks down?

It is vital to see any given person as just a cog in the machine. Think of an effective football team. Each player has a role, a set of skills. Therefore, even the greatest players can be replaced. Instead of seeing people as people, see them only as functional objects. When you know what one person does for you, you will always be able to have a replacement in mind should you need one.

The Danger Of Need

It is almost fashionable for people to rely on others to excess in the modern world. Think how common it is to hear statements such as 'I don't know what I would do without you', 'You are my everything' or even 'You are my right arm'. What an absolutely pathetic state of affairs. The modern world is actually cultivated to make people reliant and compliant. If everyone is relying on everyone else, and, more importantly, large companies, then everyone is meek and obedient. When people are unable to realize that they are in fact better off being truly independent, they are ripe to be controlled. Machiavelli and Sun Tzu realized this at the times they were writing in and it is more true today than it ever has been.

So what are some of the main ways in which reliance on people or things outside of ourselves is dangerous? Let's look at a few examples, both applying to personal and external leadership, and explore ways in which the disease of dependency can be defeated and overcome.

In the context of company leadership, lacking the ability to carry out an essential part of a process in-house is a mistake. This is a controversial statement to make as often the modern approach is to outsource almost everything possible. Outsourcing has a time and place but it should be a consciously chosen decision rather than an automatic assumption. Also, it is always useful to have people within an organization who are capable of carrying out every aspect of the company's core processes, even if these aspects are usually handled by outsourcers. Why?

If you rely on a particular skill or ability as part of your business, but do not have anyone capable of carrying it out in-house, then you are always at the mercy of others. Yes, there are an abundance of freelancers available at any time of day with the click of a mouse. However, relying on such people is a recipe to always have terms and conditions dictated to you. If you have someone within your direct control who is capable of carrying out what you need doing, then you will always be in a stronger position. You always should aim to be the source that other people rely on, rather than relying on others.

Personal Strength

The idea of independence as strength is also as applicable to individuals as it is to companies and other large organizations. There are several areas in which it is wise to cultivate strong, independence self-reliance - finance, health, skill and education. Let's look at each of these in turn.

Financial self-reliance is an absolutely vital source of strength in the modern world. There are several ways in which this can be utilized. The first factor is to be as free of debt as possible. Debt is effectively slavery. Sadly, debt is the modern norm. A lot of modern households have loan and credit card debts as well as a crippling mortgage. This traps people into jobs they may not really want to work, relationships they may not want to be in and places they don't really want to live in. Debt is a burden, an anchor and a vampire. It keeps people stuck in one place and saps them of their energy, vitality and financial freedom. The first step to achieving strength through independence is to get out of every kind of debt.

Another aspect of financial self-reliance is to have skillsets which will always be able to generate income at any time and place. This stops people being reliant on any given company or any given set of circumstances in order to generate income. Even the biggest companies can fail and there is no such thing as a job for life anymore. Failing to cultivate skills which can be used in any situation to make sufficient income is a huge mistake and obstacle to overcome on the path to strength through independence.

Thankfully, it is easier than ever to generate independent income in the modern world. Anyone with a laptop, a brain and a work ethic can make money anywhere in the world. Think about the freedom and strength that comes with knowing you can make enough money to live your life with nothing more than a computer and an internet connection. It stops you from ever having to do anything you don't want to again. You will never again feel trapped or stuck in one place.

The final component to financial strength through independence is to build up reserves of cash and to cultivate a long-term approach to financial planning. Many people live only in the short-term and do not think ahead. People assume the way things are will always stay the same and there is no chance of a crisis or disruption to make their lives uncomfortable. It is absolutely vital to build up financial reserves in two main areas - immediate access to cash reserves to handle short term crises, and long-term financial plans to protect against the future.

Taking a proactive, independent approach to our own health is another vital component of achieving strength through independence. Many people take the view of relying on doctors, medication and the pharmaceutical industry in order to get by in life. What people often fail to realize is that we can often handle our own health more cheaply and effectively than relying on others. For example, many of the major health problems of our time can be dealt with through simple solutions such as eating healthy, natural food and enjoying some exercise in the fresh air. Realizing that good health is within your own grasp is a more source of personal strength.

Education is the final main area in which it is possible to generate strength through independence. It is possible now to learn almost everything there is to know from the comfort of your own home. Every book, every skill and every area of knowledge is available online. People can network and meet others at their own convenience virtually. This frees people from reliance on traditional educational institutions and the high costs that are often associated with such places. When you realize the immense power of unlimited knowledge is within your grasp then you become intellectually free and strong.

Strength Is From The Head, Not The Heart

All of the ways in which strength has been explored in this chapter come down to one key criteria - cold rationality. The romantic, warm notions of tradition and sentiment have to be discarded if a leader is to truly become strong and superior. Strength needs to always come from a cold place of rationality and calculation rather than allowing emotion or any other weak factor to influence decision making.

To make the most of these ideas, always seek to increase your self-reliance and decrease the ways in which you depend on anything outside of yourself. This is as true for your personal life as it is for your professional. Needing anything other than yourself in life is a recipe for utter disaster and ruin. Machiavelli and Sun Tzu both knew this and so should you.

Chapter 7 - Know What Is Necessary

One of the key aspects of achieving aims and objectives that features throughout the thought of both Sun Tzu and Machiavelli is the need to 'know what is necessary' and to 'always aim for victory'. This simple sounding advice is actually incredibly powerful. Too many modern leaders are stuck in the trap of not having a clear ultimate aim and not understanding what is and isn't essential to what they are trying to do. In this chapter various aspects of achieving victory no matter what will be explored and expanded upon.

<u>Win Without Fighting</u>

In The Art of War, Sun Tzu states that the best victories are those that are achieved without fighting. What exactly does this mean? Basically, Sun Tzu is emphasizing that the only thing that matters is achieving an outcome, and achieving it with the least amount of effort possible is the best possible way of doing so. This might sound like common sense. After all, who doesn't want to succeed, and to do so with the minimal amount of expenditure? If you look closely at the idea, however, you will see that many modern leaders prefer the effort rather than the outcome.

How many companies have more staff than they need? How many projects are planned haphazardly and without the strict principles of tightly controlled project management to ensure they progress in the most efficient and rapid way possible? These are all signs that many people are in love with fighting rather than with victory. This is as true in the professional field as it is in the personal.

One way of thinking about this concept is through the saying 'work smart, not hard'. This basically means that you should always set out to achieve your aims through the most efficient way possible. Being busy and putting in long hours is often not the best way to get things done. There are usually quicker and more efficient ways of execution which allow people to achieve their objectives in less time and with less effort expended.

People's personal lives are another area in which it is always better to 'win without fighting' if possible. Let's think about the idea of personal fitness and health, for example. Being healthy and radiating vitality through one's physical self is an essential aspect of leadership. But people often go about this in the wrong way, eating and exercising haphazardly and without a thorough process of logic and understanding of what it is they are doing. Often, the same amount of outcome can be achieved with a lot less effort. The Pareto Principle, or 80/20 concept, is a key way of 'winning without fighting'.

What exactly is the Pareto Principle? It basically states that the majority of our outcomes come from a minority of our efforts. Simply put, a small number of the things we do lead to the majority of our outcomes. By thinking of the most effective courses of action, the ones which will produce the biggest results with the least action, we are able to 'win without fighting'. We get the same intended victory through a much lower level of effort than would otherwise be required.

Know Yourself And Your Enemy

Sun Tzu stated that effective leaders must know both their own self and their enemy in order to achieve effective outcomes. In the Art of War, Sun Tzu made it clear that knowing one's self but not one's enemy, or vice versa, would lead to inconsistent outcomes. One battle would result in victory while the next would result in failure. It was also emphasized that failing to know either one's self or one's adversary would lead only to consistent loss and failure.

The idea of knowing yourself and your enemy is applicable to topics outside of warfare. Modern leaders do not exist in isolation - they are constantly engaged in a process of interaction. This interaction might consist of leading people within an organization or adversarially going up against competitors in some way. The basic principle Sun Tzu was trying to convey was that any given battle is a process of one set of strengths and weaknesses going up against another set of strengths and weaknesses.

The idea found in The Art of War is as applicable to modern strategic management as it was to the ancient battlefield. Any given company has a set of competencies, people and abilities that are a better or worse fit with the external environment in which the company operates. Always asking the question 'what is needed to succeed in this environment?' is a surefire way to maximize your chances of consistent, strategically planned victory, rather than the haphazard, frustrating pattern of wins and losses that can occur when only one half of the victory equation is understood.

Aside from a macro, strategic company context, the principle of knowing yourself and your enemy is also relevant to areas of personal endeavor. For example, one of the key things holding people back from achieving their goals is thinking in terms of 'what has worked for others?' rather than 'what will work for me?'. People are unique and not one size fits all. Everyone has a different personality, background and skillset which means they are more likely to achieve in some areas than others. Knowing how you are or are not compatible with any given area of life is a good guidance as to whether that particular type of opportunity is worth pursuing or not.

Use Resources Wisely

One of the strategic insights offered in The Art of War is the need for leaders to deploy their resources differently depending on what is within their grasp at any given time. Large numbers of forces must be used in different ways than smaller numbers of resources. Strategies must be adapted according to the manpower and levels of other resources at the disposal of a leader.

Think of marketing as one modern area in which this principle holds true. If a company has a large marketing budget then they are able to carry out promotional campaigns in a different way than if their budget was smaller. They may be able to use mainstream media advertizing, for example. If, on the other hand, a company has an incredibly small marketing budget then they may be forced to focus on other ways of getting their marketing message across, such as through viral content creation and social media marketing. In both cases, the objective is still the same - seeking out exposure for the product or service which is being promoted at the time. The strategy must be adjusted and adapted depending on the resources available, however.

Extreme Is Effective

In 'The Prince', Machiavelli repeatedly emphasized that extremity could be a useful tool in achieving victory. Indeed, Machiavelli often stated that extremity may be needed in order to achieve victory and ensure that things were controlled in the way the leader intended. There were a few dimensions to Machiavelli's viewpoint on extremity that he spoke of in The Prince.

First, Machiavelli talked about the necessity of recognizing extreme acts which fall within a leader's sphere of control, whether they are positive or negative. He stated that extreme examples of acts a leader wished to encourage should be met with extreme reward, while extreme examples of acts a leader wished to discourage should be met with extreme punishment. By making an example of either positive or negative deeds, a leader is able to influence the population to emulate the praiseworthy acts and avoid the blameworthy through fear of punishment.

This principle of extreme reward and punishment can be applied in both a professional and personal context in the modern time. Professionally speaking, the most effective leaders are able to reward and punish accordingly to keep the morale of those they are leading on their side. One of the biggest demotivators for workers is to feel as if their work will not be rewarded, or the lack of work from others will not be punished. By cultivating an atmosphere of workplace justice, in which the best are treated accordingly, and the worst are treated harshly, employees feel as if their job is worth doing well, and will fear slacking off. Both of these outcomes greatly favor the leader.

Machiavelli's idea of extreme reward and punishment can also be applied to areas of personal growth. For example, most people are not generous or harsh enough with themselves.

Most people do not consciously direct their effort towards either achieving or avoiding certain things in life. It is vital for us as individual leaders to punish and reward ourselves. In doing so, we create neuro-conditioning which means that our future pursuits of success, and avoidance of failure, will take place on autopilot.

Another way in which Machiavelli's extremity principle can be applied is through a cognitive reframe. Instead of thinking 'is this course of action too extreme?' the better question to always ask is 'is this course of action effective?' Machiavelli again and again emphasizes that the only things that matter are things that work and things that don't work. If something serves your aims then it is useful. If something doesn't, then it is useless. Any moral judgment on action was seen as pointless in Machiavelli's eyes. Effectiveness is everything.

Chapter 8 - Embrace Chaos and Expect The Unexpected

One of the key mistakes made by leaders past and present is failing to respect the inherent unpredictability and chaos of existence. Many leaders make the mistake of assuming life exists on paper or spreadsheets and, as a result, being unable to deal with deviations to what they expected ahead of time. In actual fact, things are unpredictable and no one has perfect insight as to what will or won't happen when plans are put into place. Planning is important and can reduce the chances of unpredictability or chaos taking hold, but no amount of planning will prepare leaders for every eventuality.

Both Sun Tzu and Machiavelli repeatedly emphasized the need to be flexible, responsive and willing to adjust. This chapter will look at some ways in which leaders can make the most of chaos and learn to make the unexpected work for them, rather than against them. Areas of personal and professional leadership will each be examined to apply these ideas as broadly as possible.

Perfect Plans Are Poison

Taking too long to plan is an absolutely crazy and deadly mistake. Many, many opportunities have been lost due to those tasked with planning for them taking too long to do so. Another area in which planning can be poisonous to success is when a complex and often expensive plan is devised for an idea which hasn't been properly tested. A prime example is the many companies who spend and waste a lot of money and other resources before finding out if there is even a viable market for their idea. It is always better to plan simply, test small and scale up as appropriate.

Taking a 'one size fits all' approach to planning is another way in which leaders ensure their own failure. Some leaders are known for overly planning simple situations which require a much more straightforward course of action. Conversely, many leaders underplan important opportunities and rush into them headstrong without any concrete idea and rationale behind what they are doing.

The best way to plan ahead of an inevitably chaotic real world is to strike a golden mean style balance between too much and too little planning. There is no avoiding the fact that some level of planning is needed for almost any situation - the key question is not 'should I plan for this?' but 'how much should I plan for this?'. Finding the right level of planning for any situation is only the starting point.

Leaders also need to embrace the fact that their plans are imperfect and will often fall to pieces. Things change, variables work out in unexpected ways - there is no avoiding this. Nothing exists in isolation. Systems theory states that individual entities, such as people or companies, are interdependent on other entities and the environment in which they operate in ways which cannot be fully foreseen, mapped out or even understood. Due to the chaotic nature of existence, there are two ways in which a leader can respond when a plan does not work out as intended - enacting another pre-prepared plan, or readjusting on the fly.

Flexible Planning

One of the best ways to ensure that plans have a chance of working out is to build flexibility into them. A wise leader needs to be as adjusted to the real world as possible - this means ensuring their plans are of a type which is as suitable for the real world as can be. This can involve a type of plan which is more complex than it is linear. For example, thinking in terms of 'If a occurs, then pursue either b, c or d, based on the following considerations' rather than the simplistic view of 'when x, then y, then z'.

This type of flexible planning can be understood through the analogy of a football coach. One of the key abilities needed for success within the sport is to have a different strategy to take for a different outcome. Instead of thinking 'we will do this, then this, then this' the best coaches are able to think in terms of 'we will do this, but if this occurs then we can respond in one of three ways, and these are the pros and cons of each option'. This type of flexibility is more suited to the real world than a rapid, inflexible plan. Inflexible plans are basically planning to fail.

Flexibility can also be built into budgets as well. Rather than determining a solid, fixed budget for every situation, the best budgets allocate resources in a flexible way depending on what actually occurs. Let's take a basic, simple example. If a budget had originally allocated '$x' to costs and '"$x' to marketing, then a flexible budget would make these, and other budget categories, flexible depending on what actually takes place. Rather than being rigid, the flexible budget is intended to be useful no matter what actually happens once plans are put into action.

Is Planning Futile?

One common response to the realization that no plan is perfect, and life is chaotic, is that there is no point in planning at all. This is a hugely mistaken view. Even a simple plan that ends up working out is better than no plan at all. How? Surely the simple, failed plan represents a waste of resources that were needed to devise it? Not at all.

By engaging in the planning process, it forces a leader to consider all of the variables that they possibly can. It forces the leader to think about the way in which interdependence occurs in any given situation - basically how things impact on each other. Even if the plan doesn't work out, having engaged in this thought process at all will help the leader to respond better to the unexpected. The leader's mind will have a familiarity of the factors at play in the situation, and will therefore be able to respond to them, in a way which would not otherwise be possible if the planning process hadn't taken place at all.

Collapsed Plans Are Life's Best Teachers

One further aspect of the relationship between planning and chaos for the modern leader is the fact that a failed plan is an invaluable learning experience. Too many leaders are scared of failure as their ego protects them from seeing the value in things not working out as intended. Some of the greatest minds in history have repeatedly stated that they would not have been able to devise the things they did without failing repeatedly and learning from their failures. So when failure does occur, what are some of the main way of embracing it and making the most from it?

One technique which can be used to make the most of failure is root cause analysis or the '5 whys'. This involves not just seeking an initial explanation for why something happened but seeking out a deeper cause which in turn lead to the seeming cause. This basically involves asking 'why?' until the deepest cause has been established. This is essential in order to not draw false understanding from a failure. The only thing worse than failing is to draw harmful and false lessons from a failure which in turn seek to the likelihood of further failure in the future.

It is important that, as a leader, you do not overly emphasize the value of learning from failure. Some leaders make the mistake of thinking 'I failed at this once before, so I now inevitably have the experience needed to succeed this time round'. The lessons that can be drawn from any given situation may only be applicable to the time and place in which the failure occurred. In the future, different variables, situations and factors could be at play which means the lessons learnt previously are no longer applicable. A plan that failed at one time may actually work in the future.

Luck

Machiavelli and Sun Tzu both recognized the way in which luck played a role in any given outcome. This is as true in the modern times as it was in the past. There will always be an element of unpredictability, uncertainty and chaos in everything that takes place. Learning to accept this and embrace it is a key part of successful leadership. Knowing that, despite our best efforts, things might still not work out is an important part of seeing the world as it really is.

Despite the inevitability of luck, we can influence our chances of success. Machiavelli likened this to building flood defenses. Although it is inevitable that natural forces, like luck, will work against us at some point, it is vital to prepare for them ahead of time. Flexible planning of the type found in this chapter is one of the best ways to protect against luck.

Ultimately, an important realization as a leader is learning to control what can be controlled and influence what can be influenced. People can be controlled, as can resources. Elemental forces, such as luck, are out of control. The best we can hope for, therefore, is to influence them.

Chapter 9 - Protect What's Yours

Courses of action for leaders can broadly be divided into two types - attack and defense. Machiavelli and Sun Tzu spoke of attack and defense in the literal sense - as violent maneuvers enacted during the course of warfare. Attack and defense can be seen as any course of action which is either aimed at expanding or protecting, in any sense of those terms.

One of the absolute keys to success talked about again and again by both Sun Tzu and Machiavelli is the need to have strong defensive foundations and protect what is yours. There are many facets to achieving this impenetrable level of protection. Some of the key concepts relating to protection as a base of strength and a foundation for expansion will now be expanded upon and applied to the modern context.

Secure First, Expand Later

One of the absolute keys to putting into action the protective ideas of Sun Tzu and Machiavelli is to make the primary, initial focus consolidating the territory that is already held. At the time of The Prince and the Art of War, this meant physically. In the modern sense, territory can be seen in several different ways.

Within the business sphere of life, territory can be seen as market share, revenue share, customer preference or any other metric which can be won and lost to competitors. To use the ideas of Sun Tzu and Machiavelli, always protect what you already have before aiming to expand or acquire something else. One of the main mistakes to avoid is pursuing new conquests before consolidating and confirming existing ones.

The idea of protecting what is already held is as applicable to your personal life as it is to your business life. Excessive acquisition without protecting what is already held is one of the main problems that cause people to end up with nothing. How many people have ended up losing their homes and vehicles after losing them as collateral in the pursuit of more? To make use of Sun Tzu and Machiavelli's ideas, always think about ways of keeping what you already have in place before attempting to acquire something new.

Of course, a measure of risk is always needed. Being overly cautious is not necessarily the method to take. The key point is to treat all risks as calculated ones. Always know what you stand to lose in any situation and be willing to lose something if you have risked it. You should always have a concrete idea of how likely any loss is and what the consequences of any given loss would be.

Be Relied Upon To Be Secure

One of the only ways to ensure your own security in any area of life is to make sure that the people and things you need to succeed are reliant upon you. In the old days, Machiavelli related this to the concept of having soldiers who are solely dependent upon you for their livelihood and income. This would prevent them from deserting you should another offer come along. Machiavelli contrasted this desirable situation with the possibility of using hired mercenaries to carry out your orders. He stated this was undesirable as they would never be truly loyal and would always seek the next good offer to come along.

This concept of deriving security from being relied upon is as relevant now as it ever was. There is not a situation in which it is better to be at the mercy of those you need rather than vice versa. There are many ways of applying this in our own era.

Let's consider the modern topic of human resource management by relating it to Machiavellian thought. HRM states that people should be nurtured and developed in line with the strategic objectives of an organization. This is compatible with Machiavellianism in some respects. It is important to keep in mind that any development which takes place involving the people who are working for you should ultimately be in your own interest. Never do things for the 'sake of doing the right thing' or through some type of moral motive. Always have your own self-interest in mind.

Also, look at ways of making people reliant on you, rather than the other way round. This can involve ensuring that people's contracts are structured in a way which makes it difficult for them to leave you and go and work for another competing company. Be fair to your employees while they are with you but make sure it is very difficult for them to go elsewhere. If people know that they need you more than you need them then you hold the balance of power in the relationship. This almost forces loyalty and makes people want to go the extra mile for your cause.

<u>Appeal To Self Interest</u>

A key element of ensuring the loyalty of those you work with is to approach your relationship with them in coldly rational way. Don't ever expect people to do things for you out of loyalty or liking. This may work some of the time but is guaranteed to eventually not work. Machiavelli strongly believed that it was vital to see people as the fickle, self-interested creatures that they are and to interact with and motivate them on this basis.

The key way of getting inside people's heads from the Machiavellian standpoint is to always think in terms of incentives. Understand what any given person has to lose or gain in any given situation. When the dual principles of pain and pleasure, which are fundamental sources of positive and negative human motivation, are understood and applied in any given situation, it allows a Machiavellian leader to take a 'carrot and stick' approach to ensuring loyalty. Always think not only in terms of what people want, but what they don't want. This allows you to offer positive incentives to encourage behaviors, and negative incentives to discourage behaviors. Of course, the negative incentives should be so severe that people are forced to comply with what you want.

Asymmetric Risk/Reward

Always think in terms of asymmetric risk and reward. What is meant by this? Basically, in any course of action you take, you should have a lot more to gain than you have to lose at any given time. This is a key element of protecting what is already yours - risking very little at any given time. What are some of the ways you can seek out asymmetric risk and reward in the modern context?

If you are leading a commercial operation in a sales context, bonus and financially incentivized methods of remuneration are great ways of ensuring your risk and reward are asymmetric. If your sales team performs for you, you will make profit, and they will take a small piece of it. If your sales team doesn't perform, they don't get paid, and you lose nothing. This is a prime example of setting up situations so that you have more to gain than you have to lose at any given time.

If you make this way of living a core part of your philosophy then it is inevitable you will steadily increase your gains over time. This is because the only time you will ever take action is when it protects what you already have and stands to add to it. The cash reserves of a business, your personal investment portfolio and your skillsets are some examples of areas you should always seek to protect first before adding to.

Understand How Vulnerabilities Open Up

Imagine a leader has a force of 100 soldiers working under his command. All 100 are stationed in defense of a city. If the leader sends 50 of these soldiers out to attack, the defense has inevitably been weakened. The Machiavellian course of action dictates that it is vital to always have a comprehensive defensive strategy in mind. No attack is worth risking what you already have to pursue. The absolute worst outcome in any given scenario is taking so much outgoing action that you jeopardize what you have already worked hard to gain.

Specific philosophies of building strong defenses and misleading an enemy in any given situation will be provided in later chapters. For now, the core idea is to confirm in your own mind the absolute necessity of first defending and building a strong base before you seek to expand. Understand how to protect what you have by appealing to people's self interest, and always seek out and spend resources on opportunities which give you the chance to gain a lot more than you lose.

Chapter 10 - Consider The Consequences

One of the qualities of a superior leader that is repeatedly emphasized by Sun Tzu and Machiavelli is the ability to have an overview of the big picture at any given time and to think through the consequences of any given action. A leader should see their role as being like a chess player - always thinking several moves ahead and having an idea of how one action will either cause or alter a later action. It is vital for a leader to not see anything they do in isolation - rather to understand that it is a link in a much bigger chain. This chapter will relate some concepts from the Art of War and The Prince in this area to the challenges faced by a modern leader.

What Changes?

The first key question for a leader to ask when carrying out a course of action is 'what does this change?' Let's take a few examples to make this clear. Say, for example, a leader chooses to allocate a portion of the annual budget towards hiring a new member of staff. This decision should not be seen in isolation but rather as part of a wider sequence of events. Let's explore some possible answers to the question of 'what does this change?' in relation to the new hire.

First, hiring a new member of staff incurs costs, both in terms of time and resources. The money that has been expended on the process of the new hire which is money that can't be spent on anything else. This is known as opportunity cost. This change, in terms of a lessening of financial resources, must be evaluated. For example, could the money be spent better elsewhere? Will the reduced budget mean there is not enough money available to cover something else in the future? This is one of the first aspects of change that a leader must think about.

Second, the new hire will require members of the organization to devote their time and effort towards the hiring process. Will this mean that they are unable to carry out some other type of duty? Will there be a shortfall in productivity? As a result of this aspect of change, it is vital for a leader to have a comprehensive plan in place for the course of action they are carrying out, rather than simply carrying it out haphazardly.

Third, there is likely to be a human or staff consequence as a result of the new hire. Will other members of the organization react well? Will they feel that their own jobs are under threat? It is important to consider the aspects of a change which are less easy to quantify, such as the human, cultural or psychological consequences of any given decision.

It is not enough for a leader to think only in terms of 'what does this change?' As Machiavelli states in The Prince, what matters is not so much a thing itself, but how that thing appears. It is therefore vital to think in terms of not only the actual change itself, but also how the change will be perceived by other interested parties, and how the change will impact them. When this is known, the leader can then determine how they wish the change to be perceived, aka what type of spin they wish to put on things.

The above step of considering how a change will be perceived is absolutely vital. It is not enough to know only what will take place - a leader must also anticipate and take proactive measures to manage the perception of, and impact as a result of, any decision the leader makes. Neglecting this step is almost willfully surrendering control and taking a lazy approach to implementing decisions.

Rationality Is Victory, Naivety Is Suicide

When evaluating the likely impact of any decision that has been made, it is absolutely vital the leader does so on the basis of cold, hard, factual rationality only. There is absolutely no room for wishful thinking or best case scenario logic to apply in these cases. Several sources of information are worthwhile when evaluating a likely impact - the impact of similar decisions in the past within the same organization, the impact of similar decisions in the past in comparable organizations and a rational evaluation carried out according to the leader, or someone he trusts, expert opinion.

A good guiding rule when thinking through changes is to try and put a % probability on different impacts. This makes a range of different potential decisions, and the consequences of executing them, comparable and possible to understand. It is also important to always think conservatively and skeptically. It is always better to be prepared for something worse than what actually happens than to be caught out unaware by something which was not anticipated and ends up causing bigger problems than expected.

The Best Decision Is Often Hidden

Sometimes, it is only through the process of careful exploration and evaluation of the range of decisions that are possible, and what their consequences may be, that exposes the best course of action to take. Countless times, leaders have been faced with a range of choices, with one of the choices seeming to be the obvious course of action. After delving deep into the process of rational evaluation and explanation, an unlikely course of action ends up emerging as the wisest.

What are the implications of this? First, it is important to be open minded to every possible course of action within a given scenario and not to rule anything out until it has been properly considered. Overlooking something without actually thinking it through may lead to a worthwhile course of action being forgotten or not acted upon when it would have ended up producing the best outcome.

Second, it is important to have a solid understanding of the criteria by which various courses of action will be compared to one another. For example, in a particular situation, is it better to incur a loss of money or a loss of time? It is better to take a course of action which results in lower organizational morale or one which results in short term savings? Without a clear methodology by which to make decisions it is impossible to choose the best option at any given time.

Conceal Your True Motives

It is often useful to conceal the reasons you are making any given choice. Sun Tzu firmly stated that deception was warfare. When making a choice within the context of a business organization, it is important to realize that you may want to hide your true motives for doing so, for a number of reasons. You may want the other members of your organization to think you are acting on a more nobler basis than you are in actual fact. You may want your competitors or others outside your organizational boundaries to perceive your actions as one thing when they are in fact another. Always consider the way you want your choice to come across. There are a wide varieties of ways you can portray almost anything.

Let's illustrate this obscuring of truth with an example. Say, for example, you need someone to leave the organization. Whatever your true reason for this, you need to carefully think through the consequences. If you out and out fire them, will this leave other staff fearing that their own jobs are insecure? Would it be better for the person to appear to have left of their own volition? Or would it be better to send a strong message and make an example of someone? No matter what decision you reach, there are endless ways to portray it. Choosing the best one is the only way to ensure you lead effectively.

Make Everything Seem Intended

Machiavelli constantly states that the people who a leader is in charge of must respect the leader and the choices they make. One of the fastest ways to lose the respect of those you lead is to make it seem as if there was no intention behind something that takes place. For example, imagine you have to pull out of a regional market in which you were doing business due to a poor sales performance. Rather than admitting this decision was out of your control, it would be better to spin the decision as a planned strategic outcome.

The key criteria for how to present decisions which have not worked out in the way you hoped is to always think in terms of 'How can I make it seem as if this was the plan all along?' It is not enough to simply state it was the plan - you must have some kind of plausible explanation. The explanation doesn't have to be perfect - if you are a strong enough leader then people's minds will latch onto whatever it is you provide them with.

Just be sure to give them at least something they can use to picture you as the one in control.

Your Life Is Chess

This chapter has focused on the concept of consequences from an organizational standpoint. However, the principles are equally valid for the sphere of personal decisions as well. It is important to think through the consequences of any decision in your personal life and realize that anything you do will have a consequence on everything else you do as well.

It is often useful to have a written plan for the decisions you make and the consequences, probabilities and impacts of any given decision, and how it will lead to any other decision or impact. By making such plans, decisions become tangible, and the process of consequences is easier to envision. These decision plans can also be referred back to in the future in order to make better decisions.

Chapter 11 - Win Flawless Victories Before Fighting

One of the most intriguing ideas to emerge from The Art of War is the notion of winning before fighting. This is a very important and widely applicable concept for the modern leader, but one which is often misunderstood. This chapter will delve into the true meaning of the concept of 'winning before fighting' and apply it to several important areas of modern life. The precise process listed in The Art of War will be explained and shown as a practical, useful process to ensure your victory comes ahead of time.

<u>Inevitable - Victory As A Process</u>

This section will now contrast the view of victory that is presented in The Art of War with a more conventional type of victory that is often mentioned in modern leadership texts. Sun Tzu was very clear on his view of victory - an inevitable, calculated outcome which has been determined in advance. Sun Tzu stated that a leader should always be aware of the variables which impact upon the chances of victory. He outlined a specific process by which a leader could predetermine how likely they are to win any given conflict. Sun Tzu was keen to emphasize that leaders should only enter into conflicts that had been determined as leading to certain victory.

Machiavelli unknowingly agreed with Sun Tzu by also stating that any conflict should only be entered into if the leader was confident of having loyal forces that would help them attain victory. Machiavelli always stated that it was vital for a leader to appear strong at all times in order to be respected by the people he was in charge of. This meant that any conflict had to be carefully managed in order to come across in the right way. Machiavelli knew that any outcome was OK so long as it could be portrayed as a victory in front of people.

The way in which Sun Tzu felt a leader could maximize their chances of victory was by following a methodical process. This includes five separate stages. They will be explored in detail later in this chapter, but, broadly speaking, they consist of measurement, estimation, calculation, comparison and, finally, victory. Sun Tzu stated that each step was a process which must be followed in sequence. By faithfully adhering to each stage and doing them in sequence a leader would make victory an inevitable end product of the process.

The Reasons For This Approach

This methodical process has been chosen by Sun Tzu as the optimal method for victory as it ensures that no stage of the process is overlooked. It also gives a framework which can be applied to any given situation. By breaking the process of victory down into tangible stages Sun Tzu ensures that leaders are able to understand their strengths and weaknesses in any given area. It also provides a blueprint to map out the process of victory and understand the next stage which must be progressed through at any given time.

This approach also contrasts favorably with the undesirable alternative of leaving the process to chance. Some leaders feel as if a process, such as the one outlined above, stifles their creativity. This is actually not true. Leaders are still able to exercise their creative freedom in any given situation, just within the stages of the process. Any given course of action can still be executed - it just exists within one of the stages outlined in the framework.

Machiavellian Trust

Machiavelli provides additional detail on an aspect of victory which is not explored in as much depth by Sun Tzu - ensuring the trust of those you lead before entering into victory. As is typical with Machiavelli's advice in The Prince, he suggests an amoral approach which does not look at the moral worth of any given action but instead focuses only on the results. Machiavelli states that people can and should be manipulated into following you by any means necessary. Machiavelli states that almost anything, including acts of cruelty, is justifiable if it gains the trust of those you deem it desirable to have it from.

Machiavelli states that the best way to have people do whatever you wish is to have them rely on you in some way. This is an element which can be tied in with Sun Tzu's victory framework. It is possible to think of it in terms of Machiavelli dealing with the psychological, interpersonal elements of victory, while Sun Tzu deals with the external process, stage by stage. Two great leadership theorists' ideas are not in conflict. They in fact complement each other and blend in order to make a superior, complete understanding of victory.

No Easy Wins

One common mistake made by many leaders is in thinking that only entering into situations where victory is flawless means entering into easy battles only. This is incorrect. This victories which are achieved do not have to be easy - they just have to be certain. While this may indeed include some wins that come easier than others, it by no means limits the leader to pursuing easy situations. Situations of any difficulty at all can be taken on - as long as the leader has ensured victory in advance by carefully following the stages of Sun Tzu's process, and also respecting Machiavelli's teachings on the inner dimensions of leadership.

Make Yourself Invulnerable

The next chapter of this book is devoted entirely to a vital element of leadership and strategic action from the shared perspectives of Sun Tzu and Machiavelli - making yourself invulnerable before attempting to exploit the vulnerability of others. This will be explored in the next chapter, but for now it is enough to understand a leader must first master their own life before attempting to exploit the opportunities that life presents.

Sun Tzu's Five Steps To Flawless Victory

The precise process by which Sun Tzu states victory will be guaranteed in the Art of War will now be outlined in full. It is important to note that it is the responsibility of every leader to think of how these steps best apply to their present circumstances. What is important is not taking the precise words of Sun Tzu, but interpreting the lesson conveyed by them and making it applicable to the modern era.

1. Measurement

The first stage of victory for any leader is to measure the various aspects of a conflict which can be measured. In the old days this involved measuring troop numbers and tallying up various types of weaponry. In the modern context this is more likely to be a relatively mundane aspect of business such as measuring staff numbers, the sizes of various departments, the assets and debts of a business and any other quantifiable variable which can impact upon the operations or success of an organization.

2. Estimation

Some things cannot be measured with certainty and these must be estimated, according to Sun Tzu. It is of course first necessary to carry out the measurement step. This ensures that nothing which can be measured is left to estimation. Some things which may be estimated in the modern context include sales figures, the success of marketing campaigns, various aspects of competitor's businesses, and the general market conditions of any future time period.

3. Calculation

It is possible to quantify some aspects of success in any given situation. For example, costs for any given product can be calculated. The cost of paying staff for any given time period can also be worked out, provided that data is available for the numbers of staff on various salaries. The cost of marketing can be calculated, provided that the rates and usage expectations of various forms of media are known.

4. Comparison

In the classical context, Sun Tzu stated that it was vital to take all of the data gathered in the preceding steps and use it to measure one's forces against those of an enemy. In the old days this referred to physical combat. The concept of measurement is one which is as vital now as it ever was, however, and one which can be applied to both professional and personal contexts.

Companies should use the concept of measurement ahead of any potential new competitive scenario. One common mistake companies make is having a lack of strategic assessment in terms of knowing comparisons with a competitor. It is vital to not only measure your own company against those you are going up against - but also to do so only in strategically relevant areas. By knowing the measurable metrics that will determine victory you can see which company has the overall advantage. This information can be used as the basis for deciding whether to act or not.

Comparison is also needed within the personal sphere of a leader's influence. A leader must use comparison to make the most of their free time. It is likely that a leader's professional responsibilities will dominate the majority of their time and therefore free time is an extremely scarce resource. It is vital to compare different activities against each other to determine which is the best use of your time. This process ensures that nothing is overlooked and only the most preferable activities are pursued.

5. Victory

Sun Tzu states that, if the previous steps are properly followed, victory will inevitably occur. In the Art of War victory literally meant triumph in violent combat. In the modern context, however, victory will depend upon the situation the leader is in at any given time. Victory can exist in both a collective and a personal sense.

In order to understand when victory has been attained it is first vital for a leader to define it in advance. A clear criteria for victory must be known before any course of action is chosen. Without this step there is no way of justifying the expenditure of time and other resources in order to chase an outcome which is not clearly understood.

Finally, it is vital for a leader to set the personal standard that they will accept victory and nothing less in any given situation. Some leaders make the mistake of compromising and achieving less than they initially set out to. This is an error. If anything, leaders are advised to set targets which are in excess of their goals. This means that, even if you happen to fall short in your aims, you still probably met or exceeded your aims.

Chapter 12 - Eternal Invulnerability

One of the fascinating truths which emerges when studying the depths of meaning within the teachings of both Machiavelli and Sun Tzu, side by side, is that both thinkers emphasize that one must first be invulnerable. This is seen as the essential first step of a two step process which culminates in using personal invulnerability to exploit the vulnerability of others. This chapter will update this concept for the modern era and show both how to become invulnerable and then to turn this to your strategic advantage by exploiting vulnerabilities in your environment.

<u>Strengthen First</u>

It is fashionable in the modern times for leaders to try and do everything at once. Some companies believe that they will be able to replicate the fast growth of modern success stories such as Facebook and Uber. In reality, what many fail to realize, is that the percentage of companies that survive is actually quite low. One of the biggest reasons that young companies fail is due to trying to do everything at once. Machiavelli and Sun Tzu both stress the need to make one's own position as strong as possible before then looking to exploit others.

The wisdom of this classical stance is clear. By making sure one cannot be attacked first, it increases the chances of later success in two ways. First, it ensures that the leader is not vulnerable to attack. Second, it increases the chances that a competitor will attack first, thus leaving themselves vulnerable. This is as true in the modern era as it was in the times of Sun Tzu and Machiavelli, albeit with different areas of applicability.

By choosing to strengthen first, leaders set themselves apart from the modern trend for early and rapid expansion at any cost. It gives the leader's venture, whatever it may be, the absolute best chance of surviving the difficult early period. Only after totally becoming invulnerable does a company seek out possible opportunities to expand outward. So what exactly leads to a company being invulnerable?

One of the key aspects of building invulnerability in the area of life is to think in a long term way. Decisions must be made that look far ahead into the future and considers the strategic impact of any given course of action in terms of the bigger picture. This means executing plans that will build a foundation for future years, even if it means that success is slower in the immediate short term.

Your Own View

Your own view of the particular areas you wish to strengthen at any given time is an important starting point for your decision making. This can exist within the context of a company or within a leader's own personal attributes. There are several methods by which a leader can explore their own view of what needs to be strengthened.

One way of expressing a leader's view of how a company, for example, needs to be strengthened is to brainstorm as many endings to the sentence of '...isn't perfect about this company' as possible. By setting the standard so high, 'not perfect', it gives the leader permission to delve as freely as possible into the different areas of the company which could be improved. By first putting everything on the table the leader is able to select the points which are weakest and therefore requiring attention most urgently.

It is also important to use your own view as a starting point of ideas when it comes to the sphere of self improvement. In this area, in fact, your own view is more important than any external perspective. Only you have access to your deepest desires, fears and motivations and therefore you are your best judge. It is likely you know the areas of life in which you most want to improve. However, making the time to write this down in clear, specific terms will help you to strengthen your personal life in the most focused way possible.

External Perspectives

There is no escaping the fact that any leader is bound to have blind spots when it comes to their own company. It is therefore vital to combine your own personal viewpoint with some valued perspectives from external experts. There are a variety of external viewpoints it is beneficial to have. We will now explore how to gain and make the most of external viewpoints of your company or personal self.

One of the best ways for a company to gain an idea of which areas of it need to be strengthened is by hiring the services of a consultancy company. This should ideally be a company with a track record of improving companies within your field. They will then carry out a strategic review of your business and company culture which is likely to identify various areas in which you can strengthen. You will also be provided with actionable advice of how to turn these various areas around.

Taking the time to get the external perspective of a company's accountancy firm is another invaluable viewpoint to have. Nothing spells out the fortunes of a company as clearly as its financial statements. A good accountant will be able to make suggestions as to how a company's financial decisions can be adapted in order to strengthen its fundamental operations.

External viewpoints are also useful for a leader's personal ambitions. One of the best external perspectives to have in this area is that of a trusted mentor. The best mentors are those which are further ahead of your individual career path as a leader. By spending time with a mentor you can learn from their experience and rapidly accelerate the rate at which you progress through your professional life.

Trusted advisors, colleagues, friends and family can also be useful in determining which area of your personal life to make invulnerable. It is important to make note of the Machiavellian teaching of only taking advice from those whose opinions are truly valuable. Those you seek advice from should feel free to speak openly - but only when called upon. Machiavelli felt a leader should maintain a certain distance and not be too accessible at any given time. You can apply this idea in the modern time by being discerning about those whose opinions you trust.

Machiavellian SWOT

This SWOT framework, in which a company analyzes its strengths, weaknesses, opportunities and threats, is a classic tool of strategic management. This method will now be updated and applied in light of Machiavellian principles.

This Machiavellian SWOT analysis will be shown as useful for making strategic plans in both the corporate and personal spheres of life.

The focus of this chapter is invulnerability and, if you have carried out the advice contained within, have a clear ideas of the areas in which you and your company are strong. Knowing your strategic strengths is a vital first step to making general strategic plans. The aspects that you consider strengths may be situational - insofar as what is an advantage in one context may not be in another and vice versa.

Weaknesses can also be known by applying the rest of this chapter - simply put, the areas you are trying to strengthen most are your weaknesses. Whatever you have determined to be most urgently in need of added protection is likely to be the most vulnerable part of your company or personal life. The general weakness itself should not only be considered, but also the specific ways in which it leaves you strategically disadvantaged.

Opportunities, in the Machiavellian sense, can be seen as the attributes which make one entity or individual able to exercise power over another. This may be some area in which you are stronger than a rival in your competitive environment. It is important to know not only which opportunities you have at any given time, but how probable they are to succeed in, and what the rewards and costs of each opportunity are.

Threats can be seen as the factors possessed by another company or individual who would be able to exploit your strategic weaknesses. If your company had a product in an industry with low barriers to entry, for example, then it would leave your company vulnerable to having to compete with a steady stream of new entrants. When the precise number of competitive actors are not known in a given situation it makes it difficult for a company to plan the resources and methods needed to gain and sustain a competitive advantage.

Ever Increasing Personal Power

A leader's invulnerability in any given area of life starts with making constant progress in every relevant area of their own life. This means constantly growing in a number of aspects - finances, health, career, knowledge and any other aspects within one's personal value system. By setting different goals in every meaningful area of life, it ensures progress is balanced and a leader advances in every area.

The only way to ensure that progress is steady is to set goals through a formal system. By using a method such as SMART, which makes goals specific, measurable, attainable, relevant and time limited, a leader can always have clear checkpoints in which to progress in every aspect of their life they wish to.

Chapter 13 - Know When To Push And Pull

One of the most impressive aspects of Sun Tzu's work is that it manages to strike a sense of balance throughout. It always focuses on the duality that is present in life and does this in a number of ways. One such aspect is the repeated need to both know when to act and when to wait and force others to act first. Sun Tzu states there is a time and a reason for both courses of action. This chapter will offer insight into the process of knowing when to act and when to make others act. It will also explore the process way to understand the power dynamic in terms of potential forces in any given scenario.

Act And Make Others Act

Sun Tzu states that a leader must be equally skilled in two areas of effectiveness. First, the leader must know when the time is to take decisive outgoing action and the best way to be in any given situation. The leader must also know when the time is to sit back and wait for their adversary to act first.

One of the times where it is vital for a leader to take the initiative and strike first is when there is a strategic mismatch between your own side and your competitor's. If there is an area in which you possess a strategic competitive advantage and they possess a glaring weakness, it is vital to exploit this chance while it is clear. This requires a readiness to act and an understanding of how to best exploit the identified opportunity. As soon as the other party is aware you are acting they are likely to take counter measures. You must therefore be able to act in a way which cannot be countered.

As well as knowing when to act, it is important to know when to make your competitor act. This can be done in two ways, both of which apply key concepts from the Art of War. First, it is vital to put across the appearance of a weakness in one area, when actually you are strong in this area. This fulfills the idea that 'deception is the art of war'. This prevents your opponent from being able to accurately prepare for you and gives you an advantage when it comes to conflict. Second, you can act in a way which encourages your opponent to be drawn out in a way which leaves them vulnerable to counter action.

Vital components of knowing when to act, and when to draw others out, are seeing the balance of power between competing forces in any scenario, and having a logical process in place in which to evaluate various courses of action within the context of the power balance. The remainder of this chapter will detail how to achieve these two outcomes.

Power Is Balanced

The idea of a balance of power between competing forces is most easily illustrated through the example of two competitors. The general principle applies no matter how many entities are competing, however. There is only a certain amount of power to be had when two forces go head to head and it is likely that one company will have more power than the other. This can come down to simple quantifiable metrics like the number of workers or the financial value or to more nuanced aspects such as the strategic fit of strengths and weaknesses between the two companies.

The power balance is a key determinant of who will succeed and who will fail when two or more parties go head to head. It is important to note that the power balance may vary in different situations between the two same parties. Say, for example, we are comparing two medium sized technology companies. In one region of the world, the balance of power may tip in the favor of company A. In another region, however, the majority of the power may be held by company B. It is important to determine what is the most powerful factor in any given situation and then see which company is stronger in that area.

Logical Process

One of the best ways to know when to act and when to wait for the other to act is to have a logical process. This is known as decision mapping and allows you to foresee the consequences of any path of action. This is most effective if written down on paper. You start by writing out all of the possible courses of action in front of you. You then write down what will follow each, so for example 'if I do x, then y will occur, which will be followed by z' and so on. This allows you to clearly, visually compare the eventual outcomes of any action you are considering.

This decision map is most useful if you are able to understand it in terms of your goals. If you know what you are trying to gain, or avoid, in any given situation then you can take the decision which fits with this goal. For example, if you want to take the quickest course of action, then you can easily use your decision map to determine what this will be.

Power Isn't Straightforward

One of the most common mistakes to make is to misunderstand the exact nature of power in any given situation. There are many situations in which the factor that determines the balance of power isn't obvious at first. This means that, sometimes, a smaller company can hold the balance of power against a larger company due to excelling against them in some strategically key aspect.

The hard to predict balance of power also acts as a vulnerability which must be countered. Leaving any factor in a company, or within your personal life, weak, means that you may be vulnerable, even if your overall balance is strong. The unequal power dynamic at play means that weakness in any area equates to weakness overall. You therefore cannot allow any area of your business or life to be considered less important than any other. Your armor is only as strong as its weakest link.

Concealing Intent

One of the best ways you can increase the power balance in your favor is to conceal the true intent of your actions at all times. One of the main reasons you may struggle in terms of the power balance is if your competitor is aware of your intent and is able to position themselves to neutralize your plans. If, however, you conceal your intent until it is already underway, your competitor does not have time to prepare themselves. The element of surprise works in your favor and means that the power balance is more likely to be yours as a result of your adversary not being able to adjust.

Know Your Counter Measures

Guess what? Just as you will sometimes choose to push outwards in action and other times subversively wait and trigger action, your competitors and enemies will do the same. You need to know, in advance, what you will do at any given time should your adversary either act or try to tempt you into acting.

In order to know your best move at any given time, you need to know how your forces and resources stack up against your competitors. You will therefore know who is stronger in key strategic areas and whether you can afford to be aggressive or not. It is important to have accurate measures with which to compare. Underestimating the forces you will be going up against is one of the quickest ways to lose through a lack of proper planning.

The key to planning countermeasures is to always think several steps ahead. Don't only think in terms of what will happen after a course of action - but what will happen after that, and so forth. Often, by thinking something through to several stages in the future, what seemed to be wise will be shown to be foolish and vice versa. Nothing exists in isolation, and every action has a consequence. Just as you need to be aware of how your own actions may leave you vulnerable and open to a possible counter, you must look for opportunities of your own opened up by your adversary.

Understand that no situation is static. An opportunity can exist one moment and vanish the next. There is no guarantee that the weaknesses you identified in your competitor several weeks ago still exist. You must always be open to taking flexible courses of action and being willing to adjust as you go based on changing circumstances. Later chapters of this book deal with the idea of flexibility in more depth, but for now, just be aware that staying static does not give you the best chance of success.

Understand that push and pull do not exist in isolation, but rather as steps in sequences, for example push, pull, push. Just as you have sequences, so does your adversary. Planning countermeasures in advance allows you to neutralize threats and think strategically and in terms of the big picture.

Chapter 14 - Strategic Study

One of the key methods of improvement within the area of strategic leadership that was valued by both Sun Tzu and Machiavelli was study. Each theorist stated that study was vital for a leader to grow in their knowledge and to gain new ideas and tactics to put into practice. This chapter will explore how to make the most of strategically directed study to accelerate your growth as a leader. The importance of studying both role models to emulate and enemies to exploit will be explored and explained. The specific areas of competitive study to undertake will be broken down into clear stages.

<u>Study Strategically</u>

One of the most deceptively serious pitfalls for the modern leader is acquiring knowledge at random and in a way which does not further their strategic aims. There is an abundance of information in the modern world. It is easier than ever to read books and access articles online. With the advent of mobile technology people are always connected to the internet and there is never a time where they are not able to read information. The byproduct of this excessive availability is that people often study at random and without a clear purpose. This leads to them having a variety of random knowledge.

The antidote to the problem of this random knowledge acquisition is to have clear goals and areas in life in which you want to become more skilled. By studying specifically with these goals in mind you will be able to direct your efforts and only exert energy acquiring information you can use. Just as important as knowing what to study is knowing what not to study. A leader's time is limited and being as efficient as possible in the acquisition of new knowledge will maximize the return on investment in terms of time spent learning.

It is important for a wise leader to study actively rather than passively. This means not merely taking in information - rather it is important to engage with it actively, such as by making notes or repackaging the information in some way. This method of processing new information is easier to retain and embeds itself more deeply into the mind of the leader.

Role Models

One of the key areas for a leader to study in a strategic way is role models. Many coaches of success, such as Tony Robbins, emphasize the importance of figuring out how others before you have achieved the things you set out to do. It is important to analyze the choices these people made and how their beliefs and values allowed them to succeed in the area you are pursuing.

The best leaders are able to take role models in the areas they wish to experience success in, but not accept them blindly. Instead, the effective leader aims to determine which aspects of the role model can be used in their current circumstance and which are suited to the time of the role model only.

It is also possible to combine various lessons from different role models into one course of action. There may be aspects from different role models which seem relevant to your current situation as a leader. There is no harm in combining the best of these ideas. It is important, however, that you are sure to consider whether actions are likely to work alongside each other or against each other. Choosing compatible actions is an essential part of reaching your aims if you are going to combine multiple role models.

Know Your Enemy

Just as you must know the details of others who have experienced success in your aims before you, it is vital to know who you will be going up against on your path to success. There is no escaping the fact that the path to success will feature many confrontational situations in which you will be pitched against a competitor or other adversary. You must know exactly how to analyze your enemy and exploit them in a way which is best suited to you.

Understanding the adversaries and competitors you have faced in the path is a good starting point for moving forward. By systematically exploring your past wins and losses you may be able to determine patterns or other insights into how you perform. You may notice a way in which you commonly are able to come out on top of a competitive situation. If you find such a factor then it is wise to try it again against future adversaries you come up against.

Just as the best leaders must take role models and update them for their current situation, it is vital to take the lessons from previous wins and losses and modify them as well. Understand that what worked at one time may not work in another. By knowing not only what worked before, but the conditions in which it worked and why it was suitable for them, you are able to know which lessons for the past will aid your current situation and which will not.

When looking at an enemy or competitor it is vital to think about them in terms of the weaknesses you notice and the possible ways you can exploit them. It will often be tempting to see things through an idealized or ego based viewpoint. Avoid this. See things as they are rather than how you wish they were. Failing to be accurate in your study of the enemy will mean you prepare for an enemy who does not exist in reality. This is sometimes more dangerous than not preparing at all.

<u>The Steps</u>

Sun Tzu outlined specific steps for strategic study within the Art of War which he felt were able to determine the necessary information about any given situation. He urged leaders to consider the strengths, weaknesses, vulnerabilities and projections at play in any given situation. Each of these factors will now be considered in turn for the modern context.

Strengths relate to the ways in which a given course of action is favorable to the company or individual carrying it out. This is usually due to a strategic fit existing between the attributes of the acting agent and the environment in which it acts. If, for example, a company has a strength within mass media marketing, and they happen to launch a product at a time in which the market is especially susceptible to this form of marketing, then a strategic match occurs and the company is likely to succeed. Knowing not only strengths but how they can be applied to the environment external to the company is a key part of the strategic process.

Studying the strengths present in any given situation requires a leader to be measured in his thinking. On the one hand, there is the temptation to overestimate the strengths of the company or individual, due to a personal bias of pride. This must be avoided as overestimating the strength aspect will lead to failed plans when the time to execute comes.

Equally, the wise leader must be sure to avoid underestimating his own strengths due to either bad judgment or a lack of confidence. Underestimating the advantages of any given situation is a surefire way to fail to maximize the potential benefit of any given opportunity.

Weaknesses are the ways in which any given course of action is not favorable to the strategic profile of a company or individual involved. Just as strengths are a guide as to which course of action to take at any time, weaknesses are red flags of which path to avoid.

Choosing a course of action requires a balancing act to be drawn between the strengths and weaknesses at play in any given course of action. Think of each strength as a positive point and each weakness as a negative. The most positive final outcome is the most advisable course of action at any given time. This is by no means the final stage of the evaluation process, however.

Vulnerabilities refer to the ways in which you as a company or individual are left exposed by any given course of action you take. Often, leadership advice unrealistically advises seeking out a course of action in which you do not leave yourself at all vulnerable. In practice, this is almost impossible and basically never occurs. Instead, the more realistic aim is to find vulnerabilities that you will be able to cope with and respond to. Never blindly follow a course of action - always think in terms of the subsequent challenges it will cause, and how you will deal with them.

Projections are the calculations that you believe will determine any given course of action. For example, if you are launching a product, the number of sales multiplied by the price of the product is a key projection which determines the likely success or failure in any given situation. Knowing the right projections to make, and ensuring the projections are as accurate as possible, is a key aspect of ensuring that your courses of action pan out as intended in life.

Chapter 15 - Be Like Water To Drown Your Enemies

One of the most powerful metaphors used in The Art of War is the notion of water to represent adaptability and flexibility. This chapter will explore both the theoretical basis of the teachings on being like water and also some practical implications of them. Flexibility will be shown to be a way in which nature is powerful and how human leaders can draw understanding from this. The importance of clear perception and always being committed to seeing the truth, no matter how unfavorable it may appear, are also explored.

The most effective leader is the one who is the most flexible and understands the ways in which to modify his approach at any given time. This chapter will give you tried and tested tips on becoming as adaptable as water - and as devastatingly capable of drowning all who dare to oppose the course of action you take.

Murder Your Traditions

One of the most illogical reasons for leaders failing to take the optimal course of action in any given scenario is by clinging on to some habitual way of acting. Almost all of us have some type of habit or pattern of behavior which we have learned without really thinking it through. This is probably our default way of acting in some situations. However, does it really serve us better than any other course of action? If not, don't we owe it to ourselves to act in a way which most favors us?

The traditional patterns we have learned are usually one thing - comfortable. Comfort is rarely the circumstance which causes us to expand our limitations and grow in life. It may feel uncomfortable or even painful, at first, to act in a way which runs contrary to a lifelong way of acting. However, over time, you will grow increasingly comfortable with your new behaviors.

So which habits should you replace your old ones with? In truth, none! The entire point is there is no one set pattern of behavior which is suited to each and every circumstance. Instead, it is important to be willing to behave in any way that is required by the situation, including in ways you may never have acted in before. A failing to be open minded enough or flexible to accept new ways of acting is a sure fire way to fail in many circumstances. Instead of replacing old habits with new, it is vital to replace them with a new commitment to see every situation as unique, and act within it as such.

Trust Nothing

A vital element of personal flexibility is being willing to question absolutely everything. The conventional way of doing things is rarely the best way. Even though it may go against the grain, you always need to be willing to seek out alternative methods of doing something.

Think about how many discoveries throughout history have been made as a result of people questioning the widely accepted wisdom of the time. Often, the limitations that humanity has experienced have been a result of the mental blocks we have imposed on ourselves. Once we open ourselves up to the possibility of seeing things in a different way we make discoveries that were never before possible.

A huge part of gaining the maximum benefit from questioning everything is regaining the same spirit of inquisitiveness you had as a child. In our youngest years we found it second nature to always ask why things are a certain way. In our adulthood we do not find this questioning instinct is accessed so readily. We must consciously choose to explore everything from a skeptical standpoint.

Cultivating a default perspective of challenging the norm isn't only good from a theoretical perspective. It also translates into tangible results and successes. Many of the brightest companies are those who find a new way of doing something. Indeed, innovation is almost a buzzword these days. When you look at some of the biggest recent success stories, one common theme emerges - they all reject a longstanding conventional way of doing something and offer a disruptively brilliant alternative. Uber did this with taxis, Amazon did this with book buying and Facebook did it with connecting online.

Flexibility - The Weapon Of Nature

One of the ways in which Sun Tzu emphasized the importance of flexibility on behalf of a leader was by drawing a series of comparisons with nature. Sun Tzu stated that in nature it was the norm to be flexible and changeable. To prove this, he spoke about the temperature of the seasons, the length of the days and the strength of the weather. He stated that without its flexibility, nature would be far less effective. He stated that humans needed to be as flexible as nature in order to succeed. So what are some of the ways Sun Tzu felt a leader should be flexible?

First, Sun Tzu stated that no military approach was right for every situation. Depending on the number of troops in comparison to an enemy, different tactics were to be used. Sun Tzu also advocated different strategies depending upon the terrain on which the battle was fought. Whether a battle was uphill or downhill, or fought on solid or unstable ground, were key determinants of the right approach to take.

One of the applications of this principle is to always treat the circumstances of each course of action uniquely. Think of the situation at the time as the terrain on which Sun Tzu's battles took place. Depending on the situation of the time, you may feel that the terrain on which you fight is solid, and you are able to take more bold and strong action. Or, you may feel that the terrain is less reliable, and you would be wiser to take a more constrained course of action. Always considering situations through the terrain metaphor ensures the conditions of the time are not overlooked for something that worked in another circumstance.

The analogy of varying amounts of natural heat can be seen as another way in which a leader needs to consider their flexibility. Some situations will call for an intense course of action on behalf of the leader, requiring them to exert intense effort in order to achieve their objectives in the most rapid manner possible. Other situations require a leader to take a more gradual approach, in which an effort is less intense and spread out over a longer period of time.

Knowing the intensity that is required is something that comes with a leader gaining depth of practical experience in a range of different scenarios. There is no surefire way of measuring how intense to be - it is possible to look at it partially logically, but ultimately it comes down to a subjective judgment call from the leader.

It is always essential to keep in mind that there are more than one ways in which a situation can be approached in terms of flexibility. There is usually more than one area of action which can be increased or decreased depending on what is required. For example, when engaging in a sales pitch, a leader can be more or less intense, more or less humorous, more or less emotional and countless other variables.

Finding the right mix of actions to take in any given circumstance is not easy. Often, it will come down to having the right mix of only one or two variables, with the others merely making the process more or less smooth. Getting the key variables right in any given situation is often the key to resolving it in your favor in the shortest space of time.

Open Your Eyes Or Die Blind

Absolutely everything in the Art of War rests upon a leader having it within them to carry out calculations in a cold fashion which is purely rational and not at all impacted by emotion. This is more or less easy depending on the situation at hand and the individual leader in question. What follows is some advice on accurate perception for different types of leaders in different types of scenario.

One of the key challenges is for people with a predisposition to be emotional. Such people often have some strengths as leaders, such as being able to read people well, but are liable to making bad decisions due to a willingness or wish for things to be a way other than they are. If you happen to be an emotional leader, don't worry. There are several things you can do to ensure your leadership style and decision making process begins to rely more on cold, hard logic.

When thinking about any given situation, always seek to separate your emotional judgments from your rational judgments. This can be done by asking yourself 'Do I think this or Do I feel this?' Understanding if something is coming from a place of thought or feeling is often a key way of evaluating whether a judgment is rational or otherwise. Smart leaders should seek to eliminate as many emotional judgments as possible and constantly move towards a criteria of evaluating everything on the basis of thought rather than feeling.

Chapter 16 - Respect Every Territory

Previous chapters have briefly touched upon the need to treat every situation as unique. Although the general principle has already been stated, this chapter will delve deep into the methodology of assessing the territory and terrain at any given time and also specific tactics you can use to assess how the circumstances impact you. Although every territory is unique and must be treated as such, there are some things you should always look for, no matter the situation. One of the fundamental errors in thinking prevalent in leadership is treating the same set of circumstances the same way even if the environment is different.

Never Assume

Often, it is easy to assume that the way we imagine things to be is reflected in reality. In fact, it is vital to never take assumptions as accurate. The human brain is conditioned to have a set of assumptions we use to navigate the world around us. However, the old adage that the map is not the territory is very applicable here. At no time can we assume the way we see things is the way they actually are. So where does our mental picture of the world come from? And how can we move past it to try and see things as they really are?

One of the key reasons we imagine things to be a certain way before we know for sure is our experiences in the past. If we have encountered something previously that seems similar to our present circumstance, we immediately draw conclusions about what to expect. The danger of this is failing to realize that our past situations probably differed from our present in many fundamental ways. Let's illustrate this idea with an example.

The same person will act in very different ways depending on where they are and the people who are around them. Think of a man in his 20s. He is likely to be very different, in terms of the way he speaks and the things he does, depending on whether he is at home with his family, in the office with his work colleagues or at a bar with his friends. This is clear proof that the environment of any given situation is a key factor in deciding what happens as much as the people who are involved.

Sometimes, we imagine things to be a certain way as it allows our psyche to stay comfortable. For instance, many times when we see an opportunity ahead of us, we talk ourselves out of attempting it for various reasons. We may tell ourselves we lack the skill to succeed or that our efforts will be wasted and we should conserve our energy. This is an example of our powerful self preservation instinct kicking in. We want so badly to avoid threat and risk that we actually perceive reality in a way which allows us to stay as static as possible.

Breaking through the trap of perceiving the world on autopilot requires you, as a leader, to constantly ask the right questions of yourself. Always question whether you are seeing what is before you, or whether the events of your past are casting a shadow over your current perception. Also seek to understand whether the way you perceive something is allowing you to stay in your comfort zone, with your beliefs unchallenged. By asking these two questions consistently, you allow yourself to peel back the layers of your own mental distortion and gain something closer to a true picture of events.

It is important to realize that you will never have a truly objective understanding of things. No matter how carefully you think things through, you will always have an element of your own perception and experience distorting your view of things. This is natural and to be expected. Don't aim for perfection in this area - you will never achieve it. Instead, always aim to see things as clearly as you can. This is still a huge

improvement over your default biased
perception.

Respect Respectable Spies

Both Sun Tzu and Machiavelli recognized the
value of having people placed covertly within an
enemy territory or organization to report back to
you with information. Both strategic thinkers
made this assertion with a caveat, however - they
stated that any spy must have your full trust. You
must be able to trust their judgment and also
their motives. We will now explore how to make
the most of spies in the modern context, and
some common problems to look out for and
avoid.

There are several types of 'spy' that may prove
useful to you in the modern world. It is always a
good idea to have a person within competing
organizations that you can rely on for
information. You are likely to have to make it
worth the while for this person to act deviously

for you. However, the information they provide can be invaluable. One of the best ways to stay a step ahead of your competitors at all times is to know what they are going to do before the information is made public.

When using spies placed within rival organizations it is vital to ensure that you do not get caught out in violation of any laws. The legal consequences of violating any laws about competitive secrecy or fair practice can be severe. It is important to always be aware of the legality of any course of action you are taking involving spies. Always seek ways to minimize your chances of being caught out and have measures in place to limit your responsibility should you be caught.

Considering the motivation of spies is essential. One of the worst things that can happen in this area is following the advice of someone you believe to be a trusted spy who turns out to be working against your interests. By always thinking in terms of how a spy would or would not be having their self interest served in any given situation, you are able to figure out what may be motivating their actions.

Appealing to the self interest of spies, according to Machiavelli, is the quickest way to ensure they are reliable. If a spy is relying on you, they will act within your interest. There is no way to ensure the reliability of spies by appealing to some noble cause or ideal. Always think in terms of what will or won't be in their interests as this is the quickest way to gain control of them and the way they operate.

Just as you see the value of having spies within your competitors, they no doubt see the value of having spies reporting on you. It is possible to always be vigilant of the people within your organization and what their motives may be. Tracking their activity online can help to expose any untoward actions. If you feel that there may be a spy within your organization, it is worth feeding them a false piece of information that only they are told and seeing if it gets out. It is important to cultivate a company culture which is as hostile to this type of activity as possible. Any examples that are caught should be dealt with as severely as possible.

Local Calls The Shots

It can be tempting to forget the power of local circumstance in the modern era. Mass media culture has resulted in many people in different locations having similar preferences and customs. However, assuming the tastes and behaviors of any one local market is the same as another is a huge mistake. A massive part of respecting the territory is to recognize that every local market is unique. So what are some of the things to look for when assessing a market?

Demographics are a factor in understanding any local market, but you may wish to look beyond traditional measures, such as age or ethnicity.

Instead, you may want to group buyers in terms of their behavior, such as frequent spenders or those who shop around carefully. Understanding the type of buyer motivation prevalent in any market is a key component of being able to reach that market.

A local market may also show a preference for a product, or range of products, that does not reflect the wider national trend. If so, it should be sought to service this market in terms of its specific, unique preference where possible. For example, stock levels should reflect the local demand patterns, rather than going with the national trend.

No Right, Only Right Now

One of the key philosophical distinctions made by Machiavelli is that there is no 'right' - only 'right now'. Ultimately, there is no right or wrong or good or bad. Instead, there is only what works at the time. Implementing this understanding requires several things from a leader.

First, a leader must respect the fact that morality plays no part in their decision making. A leader's only responsibility is to act effectively. Conventional notions of ethical or unethical conduct are not relevant for Machiavelli. Second, a leader must never assume what worked for them on a previous occasion will automatically work again. Finally, the leader must be sure that no unconscious prejudices or biases are holding them back from making a good judgment of a situation.

Chapter 17 - Master Morale And Earn Respect

It is almost impossible to separate the leader from those he leads. After all, no leader exists in isolation. Indeed, of the most difficult and complex aspects of leadership in inspiring feelings of willingness and capability in those who are being led. It is vital to not overlook the human element of success in any given plan. Both Sun Tzu and Machiavelli offered various insights into the human aspects of leadership. This chapter contains a distillation of their key ideas and ways of applying them in the modern context. The chapter draws ideas from various sections of both The Art of War and The Prince.

The Human Element

A common mistake when leaders devise and attempt to execute strategic plans is overlooking a vital part of the process - the human element. Humans are often overlooked as part of the process of strategic thought as it is assumed they will act in a certain way regardless. This is a huge mistake. The morale, motivation and other factors relevant to the people being led can be huge influences on how successful or otherwise any given plan is in reality.

Bad planners see the role of humans within strategy as being simpler than it actually is. People mistakenly think that if a person has the right skills and is in the right situation, they will succeed. This is actually forgetting a vital piece of the puzzle. While it is true that the person does need to have the right skills for the environment in which they will work, their internal state is also a key component. People can have all the skills their work needs, but, if they don't feel motivated to put in effort, it is all for nothing.

Human beings are too complex to ever fully 'map out' and the almost infinite variations that can take place in plans as a result of the people carrying them out can be overwhelming.

However, it is always important to at least attempt to understand how different human factors can impact plans. It is better to have a rough idea of something complex than no idea whatsoever.

Comparative States

Usually, there are various ways in which you can assess the people under your control as a collective group. For example, you may lead a team of ten people. Within that team, six are average workers, two are slow workers and two are fast workers. Overall, you could say that this team averaged out to being at a standard pace. Other areas in which your people can be assessed include their levels of skill, levels of motivation, years of experience within the company and any other measure which seems relevant to the operation taking place.

While it is undoubtedly useful to measure the people you are leading, it is also important to compare this to the human element of your competitor. For example, let's say your company and a competing company are launching a similar product within the same region. By preparing the skill level of your sales teams comparatively, the motivation within the teams and the general morale, it may emerge that one company has a human advantage over their competing rival.

If you are comparing the human aspect of two entities, it is vital to compare them in a valid way. For example, if you are measuring the relative skillsets, of the teams, you would want to be sure the comparison is based on comparable measures. Someone who has years of experience in programming is obviously a different prospect to someone who holds a certificate in a programming language but lacks on the job experience. It is therefore vital that any system of measurement you devise allows for variations such as the amount of experience within a particular area.

Understand that comparisons are not perfect. Business is not carried out on paper. Sports is a clear illustration of this concept. Often, the team which is the much better prospect on paper ends up losing to a lesser team. Business is no different. A company which seems to be in a great position on paper can end up performing worse than a seemingly weaker competitor. Comparing any aspect of business is imperfect and incomplete - comparing an element as unpredictable and complex as humans is doubly so.

Loyalty & Discipline

Sun Tzu was keen to emphasize in the Art of War the importance of taking a different approach to discipline of those you lead depending on the nature of your relationship with them. It is taught that discipline can only be implemented once the people that are being led feel genuine loyalty to a leader. If a leader tries to implement discipline too early then it will work against them and harm the chances of loyalty. If people are loyal, though, they must be disciplined in order for their loyalty to be sustained.

The concept of differing levels of discipline can be applied in the modern corporate context. When taking over a team for the first time, a new leader often eases back on implementing their rules and regulations too strictly until the team has unified and people feel united with one another. If the leader attempts to implement discipline too early then it ruins the chances of team cohesion. After a while, however, it is vital for the discipline to be in place in order for the team to function smoothly.

One of the arts of leadership is to strike the balance between discipline and loyalty at any given time. Depending on the nature of the situation and the people being disciplined, it may be better to discipline too strongly or too weakly. Generally speaking, it is better to discipline too strongly than too weakly, as this is more likely to lead to a leader being feared. This chapter's next section fully explains the importance of being feared for a leader.

Respect And Fear

Machiavelli stated in The Prince that leaders are able to rule through either respect or fear. A people's respect can be fickle and difficult to rely upon, whereas Machiavelli felt that fear was a reliable predictor of compliance with a leader's wishes. Machiavelli therefore stated it was better to be feared than anything else as this was the only way of ensuring loyalty and compliance from the people.

Sun Tzu was keen to emphasize that a leader must earn the respect of the people they led. He stated that this could only come through being a wise and decisive leader and always valuing the efforts of troops in any given situation. Sun Tzu was keen to emphasize that conflict should only be entered into when victory could be assured and this belief was a key to keeping morale up and troops onside.

This principle is very relevant for the modern leader. Too many leaders of the contemporary time are mistaken in thinking that notions of loyalty or ethics will always keep morale up and workers loyal. Instead, it is vital that a leader is feared. This can only be achieved by being unafraid to take harsh action to ensure wishes are complied with. Any dissent, or signs of dissent, must be crushed without hesitation, as is emphasized in an earlier chapter.

Morale As Advisor

Sun Tzu was keen to state that the comparative morale of two sets of troops in a conflict could even be used as a valuable way of making decisions. Sun Tzu advocated delaying certain maneuvers until a time when your own troops were in higher spirits and fighting with more commitment than the other side. Sun Tzu felt strongly about this to stress that it could make the difference between victory or failure.

With this knowledge in mind, the modern leader should always seek to assess the levels of motivation and morale present in the organizations of competitors. Times of low competitive morale are ideal times to launch maneuvers and aim to gain strategic ground. Some leaders aim to take this principle to its logical conclusion and manipulate and influence the morale of both sides as per the strategic requirement of the time. This can be achieved through the manipulative release of information to influence perception. This is a powerful combination of the principle of Machiavellian psychological manipulation and Sun Tzu's use of morale and motivation as a guide to decision making.

Never Overlook

It is easy to get wrapped up with the complex strategic frameworks and Art of War comparative measures that form part of the equation of victory. However, the wisest leaders never lose sight of the fact that all plans are carried out by people. The beliefs and mentalities of the people in an organization are a direct determinant of that organization's outcomes. People can be influenced and failing to do so is overlooking a key element of the Art of War. Finally, it is vital to remember that the motivation of people should never be viewed in isolation, but rather as a piece of a broader strategic puzzle.

Chapter 18 - The Power Of No

One of the main problems holding leaders back from operating at their maximum levels of effectiveness is the abundance of options, opportunities and courses of action. The modern era has made many things possible that were either far more difficult or outright impossible in times gone past. Many leaders fall into the trap of thinking that more opportunities means that there are more ways to succeed. This isn't necessarily the case. Often, succeeding in any given situation comes down to saying no to all of the wrong things as well as saying yes to the right things. There are usually far more wrong than right roads to take so an effective leader has to say no far more often than they say yes.

Cultivating the judgment to say no to things which aren't the right strategic fit for the circumstance is one of the main elements of wise leadership. Machiavelli conveyed through The Prince that nothing should ever be done for its own sake - only to serve a purpose. The purpose Machiavelli saw as worthwhile was anything that served the aims of the leader. Sun Tzu, in the Art of War, listed a variety of different things a leader should sometimes avoid doing.

<u>Sun Tzu's Nots</u>

In a powerful section of The Art of War, Sun Tzu offers a list of decisions that a leader must know when not to take. He specifically mentions that there are roads which shouldn't be walked, armies that shouldn't be attacked, towns that shouldn't be besieged, terrains not to contest and even orders not to obey. Each of these factors will now be updated and applied to the modern context.

The ideas of roads not to take can be interpreted in both a literal and a metaphorical sense. Roads can be seen as literal directions of travel, and also as course of action. In the modern sense, roads not to take can be seen as strategic plans which should not be pursued. So how can we know which roads are worth traveling and which are best avoided?

The first essential condition for knowing which roads to travel is knowing where you are trying to get. This should be a specific outcome you are trying to make happen. For example, launching the best selling product within a particular category is a specific destination. There may be several roads, or plans of action, which would achieve the ultimate objective. Your job, as a leader, is to understand the advantages and disadvantages of each of these roads. You can then say yes to the one road which is most advantageous on balance, and no to the many roads which are less favorable.

Armies not to attack can be understood in the modern time as a number of things. Perhaps the most obvious modern equivalent is companies that shouldn't be competed with. This could be in terms of the size of the company relevant to your own, the manpower they have at their disposal in comparison to yours or some kind of other strategic advantage which means competing against them would be an unwise course of action to take.

Towns not to besiege can be seen as particular product markets which are seen as unfavorable to enter. There are a range of factors which may lead to a market being termed undesirable. It could be felt that the market is too saturated and there is no room for a new firm to compete. It could be felt that the barriers to entry for the market are too high not justified by the potential returns. Finally, it could be felt that the market is shrinking in size, or becoming less profitable, and is therefore not worth entering.

Terrains not to contest can be seen as competitive conditions to avoid. For example, if a firm wishes to compete on price, and you will not be able to sustain competition in this area, then this is an example of a terrain not to contest. Others might be an advertizing campaign war against a company with a much bigger marketing budget or launching a product to a demographic that you have no experience of serving.

Orders not to be obeyed can be understood in both the sense of actual commands issued to be carried out and advice which is not taken and followed.

Sometimes, a maxim which is usually true might not apply to a certain situation. For example, 'the customer is always right' is a well known saying. Often, it is true that it is important to keep a customer happy, as customer acquisition is more expensive than customer retention. However, in some situations, it may be felt that it is not desirable to satisfy a customer. This may be due to the expense related to their wishes or the nature of what they require. In such circumstances, 'the customer is always right' is a case of an order which shouldn't be obeyed.

An example of a literal order which shouldn't be obeyed, at least according to Machiavellian thought, is anything which foregoes outcome in favor of a moral notion of right or wrong. For example, a sales company may have a strict rule against misleading people in pursuit of closing a deal. However, a salesman might realize they have a good opportunity to close a deal through subtle misleading. They are confident there is no way this could come to light. As a result, Machiavellian thought emphasizes the need to do whatever is needed to achieve the desired outcome. This is an example of orders not to be obeyed in a literal sense.

Conservation Of Resources

The basic principle of 'the power of no' is making the most of the limited resources we have at our disposal at any given time. Although it is true that there is an abundance of resources in the grand scheme of things, there is only a limited amount at any given time. Due to this temporary scarcity, it is vital to use resources in the most effective way possible. This involves expending the least amount of any given resource that is needed to secure an intended outcome. So what are some of the main resources to conserve, and how can they be used well?

Finance is one of the key resources which should be conserved. This involves completing projects in the most cost effective ways, and seeking savings on costs where possible. Although it is good to save financial resources, the bottom line cost of materials or labor should never be the sole criteria for making a decision. Often, quality costs more in the short term, but actually saves money in the long term. It is important to think of the requisite level of quality at any given time, and then seek to attain it for the lowest price possible, provided it is up to standard.

Time is another resource which should be conserved. Of all the resources at the disposal of leaders, time is perhaps the most valuable. This is due to the fact that money can be made and lost but it is impossible to get back even a single second. There are several ways that leaders can make the most of the scarcity of time. First, they can use techniques from disciplines such as project management to ensure the quickest possible route towards an end goal is always chosen. Secondly, techniques from philosophies such as lean and continuous improvement can be used to ensure processes are as efficient as possible. Finally, time can be scheduled efficiently and wisely so that priority tasks are treated as such and the maximum amount of productivity occurs within the time available.

Resources can also be conserved within a leader's personal sphere of operation. One of the best ways to do this is for a leader to map out how they spend their time, through an activity such as journaling. This will often show that time is being spent inefficiently. By rearranging and taking conscious control of one's time, a leader ensures that they are allocating some area of their available time to every activity that they value.

Be Selfish

Often, the reasons we hesitate to say no to things and people are for fear of rubbing people the wrong way or burning bridges. Often, the only people we end up hurting are ourselves. Whether you are making decisions that will impact your company or your personal life, it is important to realize that being fearless in saying no is a vital skill. Over time, you will realize that when you say a clear no to people, they actually respect the fact you have set and adhered to a barrier for yourself.

Ultimately, we need to be able to say no to the things that don't serve us in order to be able to say yes to the things that do. Machiavelli stated that nothing should be done for its own sake - only for a purpose. By making no your default response, and only saying yes selectively, you will learn to spend your time wisely, and conserve it like the precious resource it is.

Chapter 19 - Don't Nail Your Own Coffin

Many modern leaders end up being the reason for their own downfall. There are many names used for the ways in which we stop our own chances of success - self sabotage, self defeating behaviors or self destructive tendencies. Whatever the specific reason, these all come down to the same basic principle - us standing in the way of our own success and preventing ourselves from getting where we need to go in life.

Sun Tzu mentioned five specific ways that a leader could cause their own demise. This chapter will explore and expand upon each of Sun Tzu's five things to avoid to provide the modern leader with a roadmap of perils they must be aware of. We all have immense power within us - the only question is whether we will use it for our purposes or whether our power will hold us back. Let's look at the five things Sun Tzu most felt a leader should avoid and how we can make use of this advice in the modern time.

Sun Tzu's Pitfalls - Recklessness

Overly bullish leadership is one of the quickest ways to drag a company or an individual down. It is a common story for someone to start out with the right mix of confidence and caution. Such a person exercises wise judgment in their affairs and experiences a small measure of success. This emboldens them further and they begin to see their own abilities as far greater than they actually are. Due to the fact they believe they won't experience a downfall, they make decisions in a reckless fashion. Eventually, their bad judgment eventually comes back to haunt them and they experience failure on a business or personal level as a result.

In order for a modern leader to avoid the trap of recklessness, it is vital for the leader to stay humble. If a leader has a realistic understanding of their own strengths and weaknesses then they are unlikely to become excessively confident. This in turn prevents the leader from making careless decisions that are based on the way the leader wishes things were rather than how they really are. Always calmly evaluating decisions, rather than making them in the heat of the moment, is another way that recklessness can be avoided.

Sun Tzu's Pitfalls - Cowardice

Cowardice, as a leadership mistake to avoid, stands in contrast to several of the other mistakes to avoid in this section, such as a hot temper or recklessness. Cowardice is the opposite problem - a fear of acting at all, for whatever reason. Some of the most common manifestations of cowardice include an unwillingness to act due to a total lack of self belief in the ability to make decisions. Others are cowardly due to being afraid of failure while others have not faced similar situations and therefore lack situational confidence.

No matter what the reason for cowardice, it is poison for a leader. This is for two reasons. First, cowardice is unable to produce the type of decisive action that is needed for a leader to experience success, no matter what area they are trying to advance in. Second, a cowardly leader is not one who can expect to experience the long term support of those they lead, according to both Sun Tzu and Machiavelli.

Avoiding cowardice requires a leader to have a strong bias towards taking action and a willingness to not shy away from difficult decisions. The leader must also trust in their own decision making process sufficiently to not fear failure. It is mistake to think that one's level of bravery and cowardice is predetermined. While it is true that some leaders may be more inclined towards cowardice than others, it is always possible to become more or less cowardly depending on the course of action a leader chooses to take, and their own personal understanding of the necessity of bravery.

Sun Tzu's Pitfalls - A Hot Temper

Making decisions according to the passionate feelings present in any given moment is one of the quickest ways to ruin leadership. Sun Tzu stated that our feelings, especially our temper, are not reliable ways by which to make decisions. This is due to the fact that our feelings change rapidly. Basing a decision on how we feel is therefore like building a structure on shifting sands. It is far wiser to make a decision on the basis of rational, straightforward logic, as this is more likely to reflect our longer term viewpoint on something.

Some of the reasons that leaders make decisions according to a hot temper include feeling anger in reaction to something a competitor has done, allowing problems from their personal life to cloud their judgment or being unable to separate their anger from their rational choice. Let's look at some of the main ways to overcome these issues and avoid making decisions according to what anger dictates in the heat of the moment.

The first of the stated reasons for acting according to a hot temper is reacting to something a competitor or other adversary does. The way to overcome this is to live life and make decisions according to a proactive, determined course of action. When a leader chooses to live life in this way then they are more focused on what they are doing and less concerned with the decisions of those around them. This in turn decreases the likelihood of overreacting to the choice of a competitor.

Sun Tzu's Pitfalls - Delicacy Of Honor

One of the things a leader must avoid, according to Sun Tzu, is having a delicacy of honor. This means seeing one's honor as being so high that it holds you back from a particular course of action. This can impact upon your chances of success in a number of negative ways. We will now look at the main ways in which a delicacy of honor holds a leader back and put into practice some actionable ways of overcoming each.

The first major mistake to overcome in this area is a situation where a leader feels like putting their personal reputation above what is needed to succeed at the time. For example, if a leader has gained a strong reputation for achieving impressive results, they may be hesitant to take a risky course of action which could win an encounter. Their desire to remain impressive trumps their wish to win in the moment. In order to stop honor preventing success in this way, it is vital for a leader to remember that only decisive action will add to their reputation. They must be willing to do whatever it takes in order to win each battle. After all, many people only judge a leader on the results he was able to most recently produce.

Honor can also hold a leader back if it prevents him from acting in a way which goes against the prevalent tradition of his culture or society. Sometimes, it will be determined that the only way to proceed in a given situation is to act in a way which goes against the conventional notion of honor in society at the time. A strong leader must be willing to gauge the times when it is needed to break with tradition in order to gain results. This is a concept which is supported by both Machiavelli and Sun Tzu. Machiavelli stated that the only right action is the effective action while Sun Tzu emphasized that tradition, and other orders, could be broken and not obeyed in order to produce results.

Sun Tzu's Pitfalls - Concern For Men

The final pitfall which Sun Tzu warned leaders against falling into was engaging in excessive concern for men. This has a number of manifestations, all of which must be avoided in order for a leader to achieve his outcomes as efficiently as possible. Sun Tzu wasn't saying that it wasn't possible for a leader to care about his men - quite the contrary. Instead, he stated that concern should not reach a level where it stood in the way of the decisions which needed to be made. Concern for men can take a number of forms. Each will now be explained, along with tips on how to avoid it.

One way in which concern for men can stand in the way of leadership is when a leader puts loyalty to his men above loyalty to his objectives. As a leader, it is vital you always remember that you must achieve success above all else. Machiavelli strongly felt that the only constant in life was the need to take action which resulted in your goals being met. Any relationship with the people you lead that begins to take on equal importance to you as the overall objective is dangerous and should be ceased.

Care for men can also result in an inefficient amount of time being spent on people related activities instead of other areas. A leader needs to remain focused on the task at hand instead of overly indulging the needs and wants of their staff.

Overall, it is vital for the modern leader to avoid all of the pitfalls that Sun Tzu identified in the Art of War. By applying them to the modern areas of life that affect leadership they take on a stunning new relevance which can be used as a signpost of what to avoid for the modern leader of today.

Chapter 20 - Emphasize The Extraordinary

Machiavelli was ahead of his time in many ways. One such way was his stated recognition in The Prince that the theatre of a leader's performance could be used to influence the people he wished to lead. Machiavelli recognized and felt that the people craved strong displays of leadership involving extreme spectacles and public examples made of people who chose to transgress the limits as determined by the leader. One way in which Machiavelli felt that a leader could make a public show of their power is by emphasizing the aspects of reward and punishment within the sphere of their leadership.

Machiavelli stated that a leader couldn't simply punish and reward in any way they desired and still produce worthwhile results. Instead, it is the role of the leader to find the extraordinary deeds, both positive and negative, which the leader wishes to draw attention to as examples of what to pursue or avoid within society. The punishment or reward of the deeds, and the message it sends, should act to reinforce the interests of the leader. It also needs to be culturally appropriate for the society in which it is carried out. For example, a reward must be valued by those that receive it, and the punishment must be strong, but appropriate for, the society in which it is carried out.

Don't Waste A Lesson

It is inevitable that, in the course of leadership, a leader will come across a number of situations in which their authority is directly or indirectly undermined. This is not a matter of if it occurs - it is a question of when it will occur. Seeing as such occasions are inevitable, the only question is how a leader will respond to them. In The Prince, Machiavelli was keen to show that every example of someone disobeying the leader was a valuable opportunity to send a message to the rest of the people.

If someone goes against the wishes of the leader, Machiavelli states they should be punished in a public way. This is intended to show what is and isn't acceptable and to reinforce the notion of the leader as a person of strength. There is no need to regret or hope against instances of disobedience - each one can be used as a valuable lesson and a deterrent.

It is important for the leader to carefully consider the lessons he chooses to emphasize. It is important to send out a cohesive message about the desired society by ensuring that the same types of behaviors are repeatedly rewarded and punished. Specific types of reward and punishment are detailed later in this chapter.

Put On A Performance

As per Machiavelli's belief that the only thing that matters is how you are perceived as a leader, rather than how you really are, The Prince states that any behavior a leader engages in that they wish to use to send a message should be made as public and theatrical as possible. The leader should carry out their actions in an over the top way which is intended to attract the attention of the people around the leader. This attention grabbing technique can be used to send out a message or show the leader's strength.

The only question the leader should ask when putting on a performance is 'how will I come across if I do x, how will I come across differently if I do y?' and so forth. It is always vital to be thinking in terms of public perception and how any given course of action will come across. In order to make the most of these theatrical performances, it is vital for a leader to have a desired image they wish to convey. This allows them to tailor their actions and speech to a way which puts across the intended message.

In order to make the most of putting on a performance, a leader should think in terms of what will get the attention of the audience at the time. For example, some audiences will give attention to a leader who is showing passion and enthusiasm. Others will respond better to a calm and collected leader. The point is to adjust your persona to whatever is required to get the attention of the audience at the time.

Play With Perception

In addition to thinking in terms of the type of performance which will attract the attention of an audience at a given time, it is important to think about the message the leader wishes to put across about themselves. For example, at times it may be to the leader's advantage to come across as being friendly and approachable, while at other times it is better to come across as strong and distant. So what are some tactics a leader can use related to perception to emphasize their extraordinary nature?

One great tactic to put into practice is acting in a way which is opposite to someone's perception of you or your organization. For example, if someone expects you to be confident and brash, be humble and understated. By playing with people's perception of you, you give out the message that you are unpredictable and difficult to prepare for. You will soon gain a reputation as being a wild card that cannot be accounted for ahead of time. This, of course, requires you to have an accurate picture ahead of time of how someone perceives you, in order for you to subvert their viewpoint.

One way you can cause people to perceive you as someone with whom they have rapport is to gradually and subtly mirror aspects of the person's choice of words and body language. By doing this, you create a deep sense of subconscious rapport with the person you are interacting with. When thinking of you in the future, they will recall you as someone they have a much deeper connection with than the time limit would usually predict.

Reward and Punish

Machiavelli recognized the need to use both positive and negative motivation in order for a leader to come across as effective. He felt that reward and punishment were needed in equal measure in order to encourage people to comply with whatever the leader desired from them, some leaders implementing a strict and rigidly adhered to list of rules to stick to, while others provide a rough, general outline and that let leaders act however they wish to within those broad limits. This latter way is hailed by many leaders as being the perfect balance between a controlled system and the personal freedom they need in order to act effectively.

It is noted by Machiavelli that ordinary levels of good and bad deeds need to be rewarded and punished, respectively, in ordinary ways. He recognized the value of showcasing amazing achievements or terrible crimes in order to show the power as a leader. By making a large spectacle of extraordinary rewards and punishments the leader can send a clear signal about the time of deeds they wish to encourage and discourage.

The type of reward which a leader has to use to encourage extraordinary good behavior must be valued by the society which it hopes to impress. If the reward is not something people hope or value then it is not possible to motivate them with it. Similarly, punishments have to be of the type that will deter people doing something similar within that society. In societies which have the death penalty, this is often used as an example of an extraordinary punishment. In societies without, life in prison is often used in this way.

Manipulate As Needed

Sometimes, it may be useful for a leader to manipulate events in order for extraordinary events to be punished or rewarded and a message to be sent out. Sometimes, Machiavelli felt that a leader could not wait for something to happen, as an immediate message needed to be sent. In such situations, it was important for a leader to either set up, or blame someone for, the type of situation they wished to feature.

One way of emphasizing a situation in a manipulated way is to blame someone for something they haven't done. If they protest against this, this will be seen as normal behavior, as most people stand up for themselves when accusations are thrown at them. This can be done when a particular behavior is becoming a problem for a leader and they need to deter it from happening sooner rather than later.

Think Big Picture

Leaders must realize that their encouragement and discouragement, their reward and punishment, cannot be seen as deeds in isolation. Instead, all of their efforts are pieced together in order to make a clear display of the leader's intentions.

It is vital to have an idea of the message you wish to convey overall. This is the only way of ensuring that the deeds you choose to reward and punish support and reinforce your message. There is no point in verbally praising and condemning one set of behaviors and then punishing and rewarding another set entirely.

Chapter 21 - The Ripple Effect

Sun Tzu and Machiavelli both stated that a seemingly simple decision from a leader could end up having significant and serious consequences further down the line. Nothing exists in isolation - all of a leader's choices and circumstances spring from their past decisions, and in turn, end up influencing their future course of action. There is no way around this for a leader - wise leadership involves embracing this ripple effect and making the most of it in a way which serves the leader's aims.

We will now look at some of the key concepts related to the ripple effect and how it can be understood and applied in different modern situations. The mixture of beliefs and states required to make decisions which have subsequent impact in a certain way will be put forward, in order for you to cause the most useful ripple effect possible within your own life.

Sun Tzu's view of leadership as mixing compassion and strictness - much like when a parent raises children - will be explored in detail and his teachings on what it takes to have obedient and not spoiled 'children' will be fully detailed.

You Are A Link In A Chain

Many leaders make the mistake of picturing the decisions they make, and the actions that stem from them, in an incorrect manner. For example, many leaders picture themselves at the top of a pyramid, with their orders and the consequences of them flowing directly downward. This is a mistaken view to have. A leader is in fact a link in a chain or can also be seen as standing in the middle of a flowing river. Each analogy will be explained and be shown to be a more accurate portrayal of leadership.

If a leader sees himself as a link in the chain, then they recognize that their decision has subsequent steps which have taken place before it, steps which will occur after it, and that ultimately the chain is circular and everything comes back around. This viewpoint shows that there is no clearly defined start or finish of the decision making process - everything exists within the context of cycles and repetition which may not be clear at the time.

Picturing a leader's decisions through the viewpoint of standing in the middle of a flowing river is another powerful viewpoint to take. This shows that the choices a leader makes are forced upon them by what flows from upstream and that their decisions will continue to flow downstream and impact others. This viewpoint also clearly shows that the situation in which a leader operates is fast moving and nonstop. There is never a point where things become static in order for a leader to assess them - instead the leader must make the best decisions possible within the context of a constant flow of changing information and circumstance.

Reverse Engineer Decisions

In order to better understand the interlinked nature of different decisions to each other, it is important for a leader to trace back and seek to explore where the decisions he has made have come from by exploring further back, and further forward, along the decision making chain. This will cause the leader to not only see their choices as existing outside of isolation, but will also help the leader to understand the causal links between choices they have made and activities that have taken place. So how is this done?

The process of reverse engineering a choice and understanding the different factors which influenced and caused it can be understood as a process of asking the right questions about any given decision which has been made. For example, if you have chosen a course of action, ask some of the following questions -

'What was the major factor which led to me choosing this option?'

'Which circumstances would have needed to be different in order for me to choose something else?'

'What happened further back in time to lead to the situation where this decision needed to be made?'

'What was the impact of my choice, and how did these impacts subsequently go on to impact further down the line?'

This stance seeks to understand both the upstream and downstream flow of information and influence which relates to any given decision. It is worth spending time on this process and exploring it fully - there is no maximum depth which must be gained by exploring a decision - there is usually another level of understanding to gain. Often, spending time with one of your choices is the best way to understand its full cause and effect.

Calmness, Clarity and Judgment

Sun Tzu stated that there were three essential factors which must be embodied by a leader and applied to all of their decisions in order to gain the most favorable type of ripple effect further down the line - calmness, clarity and judgment. If a leader is able to make these three factors the basis of their guidance for decisions then Sun Tzu felt that the later ripple effect would be as beneficial as possible.

Calmness requires a leader to be in the correct state of mind to make a sober and rational judgment about what happens. When a leader makes a choice from a place of calm, he causes the minimum amount of unwanted ripple in the decision making chain. Contrast this with the idea of a leader who lashes out and makes a rushed choice in the heat of the moment. Such a leader would surely set off a wide and chaotic ripple effect which may lead to unintended and unhelpful ripples from disrupting the chain.

Calmness requires a leader to detach their own personal feelings and emotions from the process of any judgment which they make. It is vital to know when logic is guiding a choice and when emotion is interfering. This comes with experience and learning about one's own decision making process over the course of time. Some situations will see a leader unable to make a calm assessment of the situation - in such cases it may be wise to call upon the counsel of trusted leadership in order to gain an unbiased perspective on things.

Clarity is a byproduct of calmness and is another essential trait for a leader to use as part of their decision making process. There are several areas in which Machiavelli felt it was vital for a leader to give direction with the maximum amount of clarity possible - in the orders given, the rules set, the roles of different troops and in the process of understanding. Let's look at each of these in the context of a modern leader.

Giving orders needs to be clear in our own time as much as it did in Sun Tzu's. This means speaking to those you are in charge of in a way which is clear and makes your wishes known. You should be absolutely explicit and give no room for misinterpretation or misunderstanding. By presenting a clear order, you give those who follow you a clear standard which they are able to meet or fail to do so. You protect yourself against the inefficiency and waste of time that can arise if people claim they did not know what they had to do.

The rules present within an organization is another area in which a leader must be clear to avoid an unwanted ripple effect. There is no escaping the fact that it is within human nature to push back against the rules and seek loopholes and grey areas. By making their rules and expectations as clear as possible, a leader ensures that there will be no harmful interpretations of rules that might come back to haunt them in the future.

The roles of the people you are leading are another area which needs to be clear and free from confusion. This is more difficult the larger the size of the organization in question. One of the main reasons that teams don't function as intended is when there is an overlap or misunderstanding in terms of who is tasked with carrying out a given function or duty. Having clearly defined team roles, where everyone knows their area of responsibility, is a vital aspect of clear strategic leadership.

Judgment is the final area of leadership in which efforts must be made to avoid an unwanted ripple effect. Sun Tzu felt this applied to enemy troop numbers, morale and territory held, but in truth it applies equally to any aspect of leadership which requires the leader to assess and evaluate something. Failing to see things as they are leads to flaws in plans and unrealistic expectations.

Understand Others' Ripple Effects

It is important for the wise leader to understand that just as their own decisions act as links in a chain, rather than unconnected nodes, it is vital to picture the choices of others in the same way. Machiavellian influence can come into play here - it is possible to lead people into making choices which may seem attractive to them in the short term but actually harm them, while helping you, in the long run. Always be willing to think where any given choice from another person will lead, and always think about how you can cause a ripple effect for them which ends up favoring your own interests.

Your Followers Are Children

Sun Tzu also felt that there was a ripple effect at work with the way in which a leader manages their troops. He felt that troops should be seen as children - therefore the approach to lead them is a mixture of strictness, punishment and reward. Sun Tzu stressed that a disciplined approach to leading would cause a ripple effect of obedient and disciplined followers.

On the other hand, Sun Tzu felt that being overly compassionate, and not strict enough, with people being led could cause to a situation similar to spoiled children. The people being led would end up undisciplined and would cause a drain on the leader's time and other resources. This was shown to be a situation to avoid at all costs.

Chapter 22 - Advisors & Intelligence

Perhaps the most challenging aspect of leadership for most people is knowing how tight to draw your inner circle and the right balance to strike between seeking advice and making independent judgments. This was an area that Machiavelli dealt with at length. This chapter is intended to be a useable and easy to understand update of Machiavelli's thoughts on seeking and implementing counsel and the right way to be around those who offer you advice.

Strike A Balance

One of the mistakes made by some modern leaders is seeing themselves as perfect and free of the need to be counseled in any way. Some leaders think that they are not in need of any input and they can make all of their decisions through their own thought processes. One of the most common motivations for this stance is due to the leader seeing seeking advice from outside of themselves as weak and somehow beneath them. This is understandable but misguided at the same time. A wise leader is able to strike a balance between getting advice in a way which does not make them appear weak and making their own choices regardless.

A more common error for the modern leader is the opposite of the above - instead of not seeking out advice, the modern leader often seeks out too much. They are constantly taking in new information and getting new information about a proposed course of action. They may value the opinions of everyone who speaks to them equally and fail to discriminate against the quality of the advice being given or the quality and suitability of the person giving it. This is another mistake which Machiavelli knew had to be avoided.

The right balance to strike for a leader is being open to the advice of trusted advisors, but only seeking it when required. It should always be the leader who asks for an opinion and input - it should never be freely offered. The leader must also limit the amount of advice they receive - it is important to be able to know when you have heard enough about a subject and all that remains to do is consider the various perspectives and make a firm choice.

Speak Freely, But In Turn

Machiavelli warned of the dangers of having advisors who did not speak freely and from their own open perspective. Machiavelli stated that advisors would often speak in a way which was intended to appease the leader and tell them what they wanted to hear. Machiavelli viewed this as a huge problem and instead insisted that any advisor who is trusted to offer their ideas and opinions must be able to do so in a way which is what they really think.

Machiavelli felt that it was vital to create an atmosphere in which any advice offered was open and honest - but only when requested.

Advisors should see, over time, that they are free to say what they really think and there will not be any negative consequences for them as a result of doing so. It is therefore important to retain the same advisors for as long as their advice is useful to you in order to establish firmly the way in which you interact.

Machiavelli stated it was vital for a leader to only receive advice when they had specifically requested it. It was not useful or proper for someone to feel free to advise the leader at all times. Indeed, being too open and approachable was seen by Machiavelli as a surefire way for a leader to lose their mystique, becoming too everyday and normal. Machiavelli stated that being open to some advice from some advisors was not the same thing as being open to anything that anyone wanted to tell you at any time.

Being out of reach of some people is difficult for many modern leaders as it goes against the cultural norm of everyone being within reach of everyone else due to email and social networking. By reintroducing a fearful distance between yourself and the people you lead you are able to ensure you are not overwhelmed with the advice you receive.

Advice Is Input, Not Direction

Another key mistake to avoid is seeing advice and input as the ingredients with which a decision is made. This is a false view. A decision isn't a result of comparing and choosing the best course of action from those which have been advised - instead advice should only be an additional perspective to compare to the leader's own.

Just because advice is sound and well thought out, it does not mean it has to be implemented. A big part of assuming the mantle of leader is to never forget that the ultimate decision lies with you and you only. You need to be comfortable with making choices and taking responsibility for the choices which you make. The buck ultimately stops with you.

It can be tempting to defer to the choices of advisors for a number of reasons. Sometimes, an advisor will have some expert level of knowledge or experience in a particular area which you do not. Despite this, do not take their course of action as the one which automatically must be chosen. You are the only one with a viewpoint that is balanced and includes the whole picture, and you ultimately know your aims and objectives better than anyone else. Never forget this, and don't be afraid of offending people by going against the choices they have suggested.

Know, Or Appear To Know, Your Enemy

One key theme that occurs throughout The Prince is the power of manipulating perception to work in your favor - this is as important when it comes to intelligence as anything else. Often, the appearance of knowing what an enemy is plotting is as useful as actually knowing. Let's explore this notion in more detail.

If you are able to cultivate the perception that you are in tune with what an enemy is thinking and the decisions they are making then you are able to mess with their process of decision making. You cause your enemy to make decisions as if you may know their thought process - this can cause them to eschew the best choices in favor of more obscure courses of action.

It is possible for a wise leader to manipulate this perception and always seem to know more than they actually do. If you make a decision which happens to coincide favorably with a choice a rival makes, then you should be sure to put across the image that you chose consciously and on the basis of more knowledge about the enemy than you actually had access to when making your choice.

Over time, you will appear as if your own course of action has been made due to sources of information within an enemy's operation, regardless of if the sources actually exist. By instilling a sense of paranoia and self doubt in the enemy's operation, you cause a crack in their armor to appear. They begin to actually work against themselves - something you can exploit to your own benefit further down the line.

Sun Tzu also knew the value of causing an enemy to second guess their own choices and decisions. Sun Tzu spoke in terms of causing an enemy to fight amongst themselves and do your own work for you. By combining the insights of Machiavelli and Sun Tzu, the modern leader should always seek to sow discord and doubt among the enemy ranks.

Strategic Misinformation

Putting out wrong information and intelligence about your own courses of action can cause a rival to act against their own best interests. This understanding can be combined with the previous idea of the ripple effect to have a seriously powerful influence. If you are able to put out a piece of strategic misinformation, it can sow discord in the enemy's process of strategic planning. One wrong decision that the enemy makes as a result of seeing things as you portray them, instead of how they actually are, can cause a negative ripple effect throughout your enemy's actions that is difficult to understand later.

Inscrutability and Misdirection

A large part of avoiding mistakes in leadership is remaining inscrutable. This involves having a tight, close circle of advisors who are loyal to you and you alone. If people are able to figure out the type of advice you are likely to be receiving, and the extent to which it is likely to impact upon your final decision, then they have a better chance of knowing your intentions ahead of time.

By publicly taking one set of advice, and privately taking another, a wise leader is able to obscure the inputs into their decision making process and make it as hard as possible for anyone on the outside to see what is happening. This can be done through making a staged performance of meeting with one particular advisor, when in actual fact listening to another entirely.

There should also be no consistent pattern to the way in which a leader uses advice. Avoid being advised as part of the same process on each occasion. Always aim to do things differently and this stops people from figuring out your decision making process - as it will change for each and every situation.

Chapter 23 - Attack By Fire

This final chapter deals with the concept of attacking with fire. Sun Tzu stated that an attack with fire could be used to exploit one of five vulnerabilities within the rank of an enemy. These five points of vulnerability can be seen as the critical areas of weakness that exist within either the ranks of an enemy or the ranks of your own organization. In the time of Sun Tzu attacking by fire was seen in a literal sense. This chapter will update and expand the five areas of vulnerability to attack by fire for the modern context and show how an aggressive course of action can be seen as the modern equivalent of attacking by fire.

Five Vulnerabilities

Men are one area in which Sun Tzu felt an attack by fire could be effective. In the time of Sun Tzu, this literally meant burning the troops of an enemy force. In our modern world, attacking men by fire can be seen as any aggressive course of action from a leader which is intended to disrupt or destroy the human element of a competing organization or individual.

Attacking men by fire can also be seen as one of the ways in which a leader can gain an advantage in their personal sphere of operation. There are often rivals in aspects of life such as friendship, influence within a social circle, or romance and dating. Know how to take someone by fire, and without mercy, using the tactics of this chapter's next section is a key way to gain a powerful advantage.

Supplies are another area which Sun Tzu felt to be vulnerable to an attack by fire. By targeting the things which are needed for any enemy to operate, it impedes their ability to do so. Supplies can be understood in the modern context as anything which is needed to carry out an operation as intended.

Supplies are also relevant to the realm of personal psychology. There are some things which people need to be present in any given situation in order to experience confidence and a strong foundation of action. By attacking these 'confidence supplies', a leader is able to disrupt the feelings of personal power and self-efficacy felt by another, and prevent them from acting in the most powerful way possible.

Equipment can be understood as the more permanent, less disposable aspects of what a leader needs to function. For example, let's say you are engaged in a corporate war with a company that produces soft drinks. The metal needed to make the cans, and the ingredients of the actual beverages, are supplies. The equipment needed to actually produce the drinks, and the logistics facilities needed to transport them along the supply chain, can be seen as equipment.

Storage can be seen in both a literal and a more metaphorical sense. It refers not only to the actual storage facilities which a rival organization uses, but also to refer to anywhere the rival leader considers a safe place that they can use without disruption. Sometimes, storage is thought of in terms of 'sanctuary', and this understanding is useful. Attacking storage by fire involves disrupting anywhere a rival considers to be a safe place, and making it unreliable and a source of discomfort for them.

Systems are the processes and procedures which a rival uses to carry out their operation. Organizations and individuals, particularly of a larger scale, are only as effective as the processes and systems they have in place. By attacking a system or process with fire, the modern leader is able to disrupt a rival's way of working and force them into operating in an inefficient and ineffective method instead.

How To Exploit

Attacking by fire is a tactic which has two dimensions - exploiting the vulnerabilities of a rival's five areas, and protecting against the vulnerabilities which may exist within your own five areas. This chapter will now look at some modern exploits involving attacking by fire your opponent's five areas.

One of the ways to attack men by fire is to identify a person within an enemy's operation that is key to their way of doing business. One of the crucial mistakes that companies make is relying too heavily on any one individual. If you identify such a person, you can do everything in your power to disrupt them. This may involve destabilizing their personal life or even hiring them away from the rival organization in question.

Rather than focusing on a single individual within an enemy's organization, it is also possible to target their people as a whole. This can be through information campaigns, such as portraying their conditions in a negative light which impacts their morale, or by seeking to make their lives difficult, by disrupting the environment in which they operate.

Within the realm of your personal life, you should also seek out opportunities to attack by fire. Anyone who is standing in the way of something you want, attack them by fire. Seek out their vulnerabilities and mercilessly and ruthlessly exploit their weaknesses to make their life a living hell. Sometimes, you will do this by making it apparent you are the source of attack, in order to intimidate them. Other times, you will want your personal attack by fire to be more hidden, causing instability, uncertainty and insecurity for the person you are attacking.

Supplies involves finding the core components a rival needs to operate and seeking to restrict their access and usage of these. For example, if a rival makes use of a particular supplier for their business, you should seek to send this supplier's business elsewhere. Anything you can do to restrict access to the things a rival needs is a vital part of preventing them from acting in an efficient and effective way.

As mentioned earlier, supplies can also be seen as the things a person needs to feel comfortable. Some ways you can attack these supplies by fire include making a person feel uncomfortable by placing them in an unfamiliar environment, forcing them to work with people they haven't worked with before, or even controlling small aspects of an encounter, such as where someone sits and the objects they use. Unfamiliarity breeds discomfort which in turn weakens someone else's power while increasing your own.

One of the fastest ways to attack equipment by fire in the modern era is by making the facilities used by a rival seem incomplete and inadequate. If, for example, your rival makes use of a type of machine which uses a certain technology, be sure to emphasize the superiority of whatever equipment you are using. This can lead to your rival becoming insecure and replacing their equipment at great cost, when it actual fact it would have been entirely adequate for them had they stuck with it.

The storage used by your competitors has already been shown to be both literal and psychological in the sense of 'sanctuary'. Both types can be exploited by an attack by fire. If, for example, your rival makes use of a storage facility in a strategic location, you should seek to take over the facility, or at least express an interest in doing so. This may cause the price of the storage to rise, thus disrupting an aspect of your rival's operation that they previously relied upon.

The psychological aspect of storage can be seen as the ways in which a rival feels safe and relied up in some areas - a storage of trust and goodwill, if you like. If you are able to ruin your rival's reputation in some way they previously relied upon, it ruins not only that specific instance of psychological storage, but also the chances of acquiring new areas of safe psychological storage in the future.

Disrupting the systems and processes a rival use is an effective way to make their life difficult. This can be through exploits on your part such as willfully manipulating their supply chain or aiming to manipulatively distort feedback on their products. If a rival is careless enough to make their systems and processes known then you are likely to be able to identify a vulnerability. When such a vulnerability is found, attack it with fire and without mercy. You never know when you will have the chance to do so again - causing disruption can lead to a ripple effect which destroys your competitor entirely.

How To Protect

It is vital to not only look for areas of your competitor which you can attack by fire - but also to see your own operation through the eyes of your enemy. You need to look openly and honestly at the areas which you are most vulnerable to attack by fire. It is vital not to gloss over any detail and instead to see things as they really are. This gives you the best chance of anticipating the ways in which you will be attacked by fire, and knowing how you can put out those fires before they start.

The human factor is one of the best ways which you can protect against attack by fires. Never rely on anyone person and never be in a position where someone cannot be replaced. Always ensure that organizational knowledge is distributed so no one person knows too much.

Also be sure to protect the systems and processes you have in place. You should always have multiple ways of doing things - that way, if your enemy disrupts one process through attack by fire, you have another process in place.

Internal and External Fires

It is important to understand that attacks by fire can be internal or external. In the context of attack, an external fire is one which you proactively and deliberately cause to occur from outside the boundary of the organization. For example, if you were disrupting the human element, you may cause a crisis in the personal life of a top performer within a rival organization.

An internal fire is one which originates from within the organization or individual you are trying to disrupt. This can occur when you are able to manipulate existing problems or discontent within an organization and turn them to your own advantage. In the example of attacking men by fire, you may exacerbate preexisting interpersonal tension within a rival firm for your own gain.